READING RESPONSE LOGS

*Inviting students to explore novels, short stories,
plays, poetry and more*

Mary Kooy, Jan Wells

Pembroke Publishers Limited

©1996 Pembroke Publishers
538 Hood Road
Markham, Ontario, Canada L3R 3K9

Published in the United States of America by
Heinemann
A division of Reed Elsevier Inc.
361 Hanover Street, Portsmouth, NH 03801-3912
ISBN (U.S.) 0-435-07208-0

Canadian Cataloguing in Publication Data

Kooy, Mary
  Reading response logs: inviting students to
read, write, and respond to novels, short stories,
plays, and poetry

Includes bibliographical references and index.
ISBN 1-55138-040-4

1. Literature – Study and teaching (Secondary).
2. Reading (Secondary). 3. High school students –
Books and reading. 4. Language arts (Secondary).
I. Wells, Jan. II. Title.

LB1632.K66 1996   808'.042   C95-932930-7

A catalogue record for this book is available from the British Library.
Published in the U.K. by
Drake Educational Associates
St. Fagan's Road, Fairwater, Cardiff CF5 3A3

Editor: Joanne Close
Design: John Zehethofer
Typesetting: Jay Tee Graphics Ltd.

Printed and bound in Canada by Webcom
9 8 7 6 5 4 3 2 1

Contents

Introduction

When I entered graduate school after ten years of teaching, I had no idea that before the year was up I would undergo a "Eureka" experience. This transformation did not take place as a result of conducting research or in learning how to write a thesis. Rather, it occurred when I met Louise Rosenblatt in *Literature as Exploration*. Suddenly, my concept of teaching began to align with my concept of personal learning and literature. My "double lives" as a classroom teacher and as an avid reader of literature could now conceivably merge.

I was anxious to return to the classroom the following year. I asked for a Grade 12 non-academic class who were not expected, as I discovered, to do much more than set up chairs in the assembly hall, deliver doughnuts, and do attendance counts for each class. I asked for these students because they were not expected to take the provincial exam at the end of the school year. With them, I was free to roam the new territory of reader response. Because Grades 9 and 10 academic students were also spared the end-of-year provincial exam, I included them in a similar style of "subversive" teaching and learning.

Our learning and my teaching evolved as I attempted to implement new and active ways of reading and responding to literature. Initially, many of the Grade 12 students, some of whom you will meet later, had no intention of participating. Instead, their protocol included "going for coffee at the café" during the first class of the morning. Not surprisingly, it took time to dismantle these barriers — both physical and mental — but dismantle them we did. By April, the students decided that they wanted to write the provincial exams, and I entered them since I believed that they were ready. All of the students wrote the exam, and all passed Grade 12 English.

How did this happen? Some of it was intentional, some accidental, some incidental. A major discovery of that first year came in teaching Alan Paton's *Cry, the Beloved Country* to my Grade 12 class. I decided to ask the students, without saying a word about the text, to read the book and record their thoughts and questions in a reading response log. For six or seven classes no one spoke. We read, we wrote, and when all had finished, I collected the logs. What I found was amazing! The students spilled their thinking onto the pages — asking questions, arguing with the author, giving advice to the characters, empathizing with them, and quoting meaningful words and phrases.

I carried on a conversation with the students in the margins of their logs. In the process, I learned I could not assume anything about what they knew, understood, or would respond to. When I handed back the logs in class, silence fell over the room; the students immersed themselves in reading their logs and my comments as though they were long-awaited letters.

What had I been doing? Despite the fact that these students were capable of reading and responding to text, I had previously engaged in a "we do it all for you" style of teaching that negated their ability and willingness to challenge themselves. This new approach allowed me to get to know my students in a deeper and more personal way through their writing. They revealed who they were as persons and readers. Above all, their reflections reminded me of what it was like to meet *Cry, the Beloved Country* for the first time. By this point, I was so familiar with the book that I had forgotten my initial response. This signified a major turning point for me — I was hooked.

When we came together to talk about the book, the students used the logs to carry on the discussion. I noticed that more students spoke and all spoke more. The scene differed greatly from those of past years. Gone was the teacher monologue. In its place was a lively discussion entered into by a number of students. I could have left the room and the discussion would not have been negatively affected.

In thinking about the process and applying it to other English classes I was teaching, I wanted to be sure that *everyone* participated in the discussion. I soon discovered that discussions could be even more effective if readers first met in small groups to share their logs. This time provided all students with the opportunity to talk about texts and their responses to them, and to come to know on another level their fellow students, thereby creating a community of readers. Their explorations probed depths I had not dared to tackle. As Dawn said one day, "When you answer a question from the teacher, it's either right or wrong, but when you write your own questions, you can go really deep. Sometimes, we can be a lot deeper than the teacher." I was now a staunch supporter of connecting writing to talking and to moving from a personal to communal exploration of literature.

Some years after this experience, Jan Wells and I team-taught a university course for teachers of language arts/English. Jan had previously written *Read It in the Classroom* with Linda Hart-Hewins and had long used response journals in her classes. Our collaboration generated an excitement about teaching that led to the creation of this book. While we have written much of the book in first-person voice, we share its philosophies and strategies, and the book is very much a joint creation.

We suggest strategies for the English classroom that invite readers to interact in personal and meaningful ways with literature. As well, we explore a variety of ways in which students and teachers together can use writing and talking as tools for thinking about how we read.

Writing and talking, essential elements of the response process, are overt acts of thinking and learning — we can see them and we can hear them. Through our notes, questions, mental maps made concrete on the page, and other informal writings, the half-formed images that occur to us as we read are gently pushed into the open. Writing not only records our thoughts, it helps to generate them. As we share our writing with others, we find through talk that our ideas shift and our interpretations grow, consolidate, and become more defined.

After tackling issues through writing and talking, students are prepared to commit their ideas to a finished product. These products will be much improved if we allow students to first focus on the processes in which they have engaged as they explored the text. Because aspects of English are interrelated, we need to be constantly aware of how and when to help students see and make connections as they read, write, and talk.

In our view, the English class is a community in which individually and collaboratively readers make sense of what they read, and reach new understandings through the exploration of a variety of texts. As teachers, it is often hard for us to accept that we do not own the meanings that our students bring to the texts they read. This may be due in part to the fact that, as students, we were often taught to find the hidden meaning in literature and to write essays that reflected the content of our teachers' lectures.

Fortunately, much has changed in the field of literature study and we have modified our teaching practices to reflect this new knowledge. Literature circles and response journals, for example, reflect what we know of how readers make sense of text. This book explores some of those practices and suggests ways in which you can incorporate interactive response-based approaches in your classroom. Setting aside the traditional search for right answers we ask instead, "How can we build meaning together?" Our students, of all ages and abilities, have taught us how to do this.

Suggestions are presented in genre units — short stories, novels, poetry, drama, and an integrated unit. Each chapter presents activities that reflect a natural progression from reading *dependence* to *independence*. It is our intention to offer you a range of strategies so that you may select those best suited to your curriculum and to your students' needs. The one factor that remains constant through all of the strategies is a student-centered focus. Take the strategies and make them your own.

Chapter One details an overview of how to establish a response-based classroom, from introducing students to the form and function of a reading response log through assessing and evaluating students' work. Like any program, assessment and evaluation play an important role. We provide an overview of how to assess and evaluate students' work and provide, in the ensuing chapters, examples of strategies you can employ in your class specific to each unit.

This book is based on our experiences in engaging communities of readers in literary texts. How fortunate we teachers of English are when we can spend our days doing what we love to do — reading, writing, and talking about literature.

CHAPTER ONE

Establishing a Community of Readers

To set the context for this chapter, I would like to veer somewhat off topic and describe my experiences when presenting workshops to English teachers. Typically, I begin by asking participants to first think and then write about their personal reading — whether they read for pleasure on a regular basis; if they prefer one genre more than another; or if they tend to read books by favorite authors or on favorite topics. Finally, they write about a novel they have read recently and why they are motivated to read.

I often post their responses on the board to demonstrate the range and diversity of readers in the group.

escape   relaxation   pleasure   go outside myself
stimulation   find out about the way other people live
relate to my own life   excitement   go to places I've never been
consolation   extend my experience   get into other people's skins
identification with people and situations

Some enjoy classics, others historical novels, romance novels, biographies, short stories, or magazine articles. The novel, though, wins hands down over other forms of literature.

We then talk about what we want to do after we've read a great book. Responses usually include:

talk about it   pass it on to another reader   savor it
write about it   recommend it to a friend   connect it to real life
form mental pictures and images   read another by the same author
do nothing with it   re-read it   write a letter to someone about it
watch the video   reflect   read more in the same genre

No matter how large or diverse the group, no one has suggested rushing off to answer ten comprehension questions or writing an essay on the main character (even more unlikely). Participants tend to mention spending time thinking about the book and talking about it with others. As readers, we all need to clarify issues that puzzled us; debate the choices that characters (or the author) made; and hypothesize about the way the novel ended and how it might have been different.

Literature: Beyond Words on a Page

We all come to a text with unique life and reading experiences that color our perceptions of the literary worlds we enter. This reality becomes clear in our classes and in workshops. Responses are filtered through the grid of personal experiences; hence, each response is unique. Louise Rosenblatt (1938) states that when text and reader meet, a unique and personal experience is born. A transaction occurs that involves more than a simple interaction between text and reader. Unlike informational texts that we act on (e.g., a recipe, instructions), literature is an aesthetic experience.

As a fellow reader, I invite students to join me in the venture of reading. I both affirm and insist on the place of personal response to the text as a beginning point. Writing in a log enables us to hold an interactive conversation with the text while talk with others helps reshape and extend our understanding. I value the voices of students who inform me of their encounters with the text. Our classroom looks much like a book club with members who share, discuss, argue, defend, and change their perceptions as they interact with others. Interpretation is a dynamic, co-operative process that has students reading, writing, and talking about literature.

The journey I have taken in coming to terms with the literature curriculum in my classes has been neither linear nor smooth. What it has always entailed, however, is the creation of contexts where readers can willingly suspend disbelief and enter a literary world where they are free to respond — to laugh, to worry, to cry, to marvel, to predict, or to be afraid — and to have what Louise Rosenblatt calls the "lived-through experience." In all of this, I have taken to heart the idea that the choices I make about how literature is treated rests squarely on my beliefs about literature, reading, learning, student readers, and my role as a teacher. The view I take of literature informs my practice as a teacher.

Who Are the Readers in Our Class?

When a new group of students arrives in my class, I want to get to know them as people and as readers. Who reads regularly? What do they read and how do they make these choices? Are they eager or reluctant readers? Do they find reading an enriching experience, or do they find it irrelevant? I also want them to think about themselves as readers and to talk about their reading with others. Consequently, one of the first items of business is to ask the students to complete a set of surveys that focuses on their reading habits in general, and on reading literature in particular.

To set the stage, students complete the following surveys. I assure them there are no right answers, and that the sole purpose of the surveys is to provide an indication of where and who they are as readers. After completing each survey, students first form small groups and discuss their reading with two or three others before coming together as a class to talk about the general results of the surveys. Sometimes, I post these results on the board, letting students know such facts as 21 out of 27 students

---

A GENERAL READING SURVEY

Answering the following questions will help you to determine your attitude to reading. Record your responses in your log.

1. Do you enjoy reading? On a scale of 1 (very little) to 5 (very much), where do you place yourself?
2. How often do you read? On an average day, how much time do you spend reading?
3. What do you like to read (e.g., magazines, newspapers, comic books, novels, information books)? List what you like to read in order of preference.
4. What do you look for in a good book?
5. How do you find out about books you might like to read?
6. Do you consider yourself a good reader? What makes a good reader? What sorts of things do good readers do?
7. What do you do if you come to something you can't read or don't understand?
8. How would you encourage someone who didn't like reading, or who felt that she or he was not a good reader? What help would you give?

---

in their class "always" or "often" have a book "on the go." Students are interested in these results, which confirms my belief that reading plays a bigger role in their lives than we realize.

READING LITERATURE

Think about yourself as a reader of literature. Answer each question honestly and thoroughly in your log. There are no right or wrong answers.

1. Are you currently reading a novel? If so, what is its title? If not, when was the last time you read a novel?
2. What kinds of literature do you enjoy reading (e.g., mystery, horror, science fiction, romance, detective, spy, or war novels, poetry, short stories)?
3. Do you have a favorite author?
4. What is the best book you have ever read?
5. What do you do after you have read a good book? What would you like to do after you have read a good book?
6. How do you feel about the literature you read on your own time? Why?
7. How do you feel about the literature you read in school? Why?
8. Do you have enough time for personal silent reading in English class? How much time is reasonable?
9. What advice would you give to a teacher of English regarding the reading of literature? What can she or he do to help you learn? What should an English teacher avoid doing in class?
10. Do you have other comments you would like to make about reading literature?

TRACKING YOUR READING

Record the amount and type of reading that you do at home and at school for one week. Include everything that involves reading (e.g., television guide, instructions, recipes, novels, homework). Begin to track your reading immediately. Bring the completed survey to class next week for discussion.

Date	Title	Time started	Time ended	Pages

Once students have completed and discussed the surveys, ask them to write about what they have learned about themselves as readers. How do they view reading? How do they compare to other readers in the class? What goals can they set for themselves? Think about suggestions for reading and literature that you can provide for the students. This sets the stage for reflective reading, writing, and thinking, a fundamental basis for teaching literature.

Each year, I collect the surveys, read them, and place them in files, one for each student. These files become my portfolios that may contain notes on student performance, copies of various log entries, and copies of other material produced in class. I then begin to situate this class of readers in a dynamic and challenging context where what we do together as readers is informed by what I observe from their personal reflections.

The basis of this book rests on the use of writing and talking in the reading process, and is grounded in the belief that reading is both a private and a social act. Writing is collected in logs and used as a basis for discussions in both small and large groups.

Introducing the Reading Response Log

The reading response log, which for the sake of brevity we refer to as the log, is a record of thinking about a piece of literature, from initial thoughts and questions through discoveries and understandings. Writing includes notes and lists as well as fully developed paragraphs. Diagrams are included, as are family trees, sketches, and charts. Given the wealth of material a log will eventually include, a loose-leaf binder provides the most flexibility since it can accommodate any number of pages.

The most important function of a log is to serve as a place where readers make overt those thoughts and feelings usually hidden in the act of reading; in other words, it makes explicit what is implicit. The log becomes a forum for expressing thoughts about reading experiences.

Why is writing about thinking so crucial to this process? Why not just talk? Much research attests to the fact that few students contribute regularly to class discussion. Watson (1987) and others found that only about five or six students out of 30 regularly contributed to class discussions. We know that students who have not even read a book are able to answer some of our questions. One student, Shannon, pointed out that by "skimming over it [the text] to get the important facts when the teacher is talking" anyone can get the answer. Most simply sit passively while the few "regulars" answer our questions. The point is, however, to get *all* readers involved in reading! Writing, unlike talking, insists upon a high level of participation in that each reader is required to express his or her thinking on paper. Writing prepares students, like a rehearsal, for the talk that is to come.

The act of writing is "thinking on paper" (Berthoff, 1981; Emig, 1983; Langer & Applebee, 1987). Readers can monitor and objectify their responses, and in the process change, modify, or reassemble their ideas — all before going public! Having recorded their thoughts, students can talk about what they have read and substantiate their interpretation and opinions with evidence from their lives.

Readers who record their thoughts, as Tammy said, "[have] to concentrate more. And because you're concentrating, you're learning. Because there's no way you could write anything down if you weren't concentrating!" Keeping a log forces readers to actively engage with a text. Once on paper, readers can trace their own growing and developing response to any piece of literature. The log charts for them the way their thinking changes.

The log gives evidence of thinking, a "window" into a reader's mind, allowing us to get to know our readers personally. The responses we collect also provide the raw materials for extensions or elaborations — any polished piece for publication — that follow reading.

Although the log is a personal tool, students must understand that it is also used for group discussions. A log is not a private journal: other students may read it and write in it on occasion and you, as the teacher, certainly will. If students want to communicate privately in writing to you, which can occur when literature is shared and deeply felt memories are evoked, then suggest to them that they use another journal for recording personal thoughts and reactions. The log must always be considered a public document.

One powerful benefit of the writing and thinking that students do in a log is the potential for using the writing as "text for talk." The logs can be used and shared to establish and maintain an active community of readers, in effect, a book club. Having had time to read and think in a log prepares readers for the discussions that follow, and provides for a depth and diversity unavailable through a discussion that has no previous basis in writing. Connecting reading and writing to talking about and listening to a text joins all elements of language in the quest for learning and enjoying literature.

The Reading Response Log: A Guide for Students

The following pages supply answers to oft-asked questions regarding logs and their use in the English classroom. You may wish to supply students with this material to help them understand the role of the log in the literature program and how they are to use it. They can paste the pages in the front of their log for easy reference.

A USER'S GUIDE TO THE READING RESPONSE LOG

What is a reading response log?

The log is an effective way to keep a record of your reading responses — positive or negative, sure or unsure. It offers you a chance to respond personally, to ask questions, wonder, predict, or reflect on the characters, events, or language of a text. As you read, take some time to record your observations. You may do this as ideas strike you or after you have read a small portion of the text, for example, ten pages. Typically, you should not read more than this amount before you write.

How long should the entries be?

There is no set length for the entries that you write. Sometimes you will want to write only three or four lines; at other times, you will want to write much more. While length is not important, what is important is that you write often and record as many of your first observations as possible.

What kinds of things should I be writing?

Although it may be difficult at first, do not summarize what has happened in the story. Instead, record your responses to the text. Do you have questions about what has happened? What about the characters? Are they believable? Is there something about the story that makes you feel a certain way — happy, sad, anxious, embarrassed? When you write in your log, think about how you responded to the text, rather than retelling what the author has written.

On some occasions, I will ask you to respond to specific questions, for example: How do you feel about a character's actions? What predictions do you have? What confuses you in this reading? What questions would you ask the character/ author about this? On a scale of 1 (low) to 5 (high), how would you rate this text? Why?

If you're having trouble getting started, use the following lines to begin your entry. Use a line only if it applies to what you've noticed in your reading.

I was impressed by...
I noticed that...
I wonder about...

Some questions I have are...
I don't understand...
I now understand why/how/what...
Something I noticed/appreciate/don't appreciate/wonder
   about is...
I predict...
An interesting word/sentence/thought is...
This part of the story makes me feel...
This reminds me of...
I never thought...
I was surprised by...

What is the right response?

Each novel, story, or poem you read will be different, and
each person who reads it will have a different response. The
log helps you to trace your response as it develops. Its purpose is not to test your knowledge but to help you reflect on
your reading through writing. Sometimes people will write
about the same things, most times they will not. Since we
have all had different experiences, we all react to a text in
our own unique way. No one else has had your experience.
As a result, no one will have the exact response you have to
a text so the entry you write will be unique. The responses
you make in a log will not be marked right or wrong.

Are logs meant to be private?

No. A log is not a personal diary. I will read it and so will
other students. You will be talking about what you have
written, and your discussions will help you get more from
a text you are reading or listening to. After you have heard
the ideas of others, you may change your mind or add to
original ideas you recorded in your log. Think of your log
as an ongoing written conversation with yourself that
others will occasionally listen to.

What about grammar and spelling?

Do your best. The most important thing is to record your
responses to the text. Try to write clearly so that others may
read your writing, and be sure to date each entry in your log.

What will you do with my log?

I will collect your log regularly and will "talk" to you in the margins so please leave space for me to write. Reviewing your log tells me something about your reading experience — your questions, observations, and understanding of the text. Reading your log, as well as those of your classmates, helps me to decide how to proceed and also provides a context for personal conferences.

You will share your log in small groups where you will have the chance to confirm, clarify, and modify your responses through discussion. As you hear what others say, you can add to your own writing. Finally, you can share the writing you have done as part of your group with the rest of the class.

Will you evaluate my log?

You will be evaluated on the quality of work in your log. Your commitment, the frequency of your responses, and the thoughtfulness of your writing will all contribute to the overall mark that you earn at the end of each unit. Your ideas — your responses — will *not* be judged right or wrong.

Group Talk About Texts

Benefits of a log grow exponentially with opportunities to use it for discussion, particularly in small groups. The logs become texts for talk: the voice projected in the log becomes a part of directed and richer discussions because readers are fully prepared for the talk.

When we examine the relationship between talk and learning, it's easier to understand the importance of talk in the literary experience (Jones, 1988; Barnes & Todd, 1995; Cazden, 1988). Talk is social and interactive — it tests our ideas and helps reshape them. Like adults, students need time to talk about their experience of text. Together, they navigate literary territory using what Douglas Barnes (1992) calls "exploratory talk." Through this, readers accommodate and assimilate their new and growing response to the literature. If learning is to be maximized, talk has to be a part of the process.

When I ask students how discussion fits into the reading process, their response typically echoes that of Travis and Benny. "When you've got other people asking you questions, you've kind of got to challenge yourself and think things through" [Travis] and "When you talk about these things you can get a lot deeper and farther into the book." [Benny]

In classes, many readers enjoy hearing responses similar to their own because it affirms their thinking. Conversely, they also enjoy hearing different responses because it challenges them. They listen to opinions and interpretations they had not thought of and can share their view with others who may or may not be of a similar mind. This exchange of ideas helps to tie loose ends. The process is a comforting one, and allows readers to revisit the text to test and confirm their initial response.

Talking about literature has additional benefits. Readers get to know other readers — their insights, visions, questions, and views of the world. At the same time, responsibility for carrying the discussion rests squarely on the shoulders of individual readers. The whole group benefits if each member comes prepared with a written reflection. When groups are rotated so that all students have a chance to work together, the talk builds and bonds a community of readers.

The closer the bond between the elements of language — reading, writing, talking, listening — the stronger the potential for learning and thinking. Writing about reading and talking about reading and writing engage readers actively and meaningfully in the process of becoming "response-able" readers.

Assessment and Evaluation: Tracking the Learning

In a response-based program, assessment and evaluation strategies must be planned and shared with students from the outset. As a teacher, you need to know what components of work and performance you will monitor as well as the relative importance of each component; the students need to know what is expected of them and how they will be marked. When I plan activities and assignments, I want to be clear about the criteria I use for evaluation, and I want to share and sometimes develop these criteria with my students.

Evaluation, for most teachers, is at best a conundrum. We have to prepare reports regularly and that means assigning grades. If we abandon traditional assignments and methods of grading, how can we defend the mark we assign on a report card? We must know that our students' behaviors, attitudes, and engagement with literature are progressing, and we are accountable for communicating that progress to both students and their parents. How can we know? How can we measure progress and how can we tell whether students are finding a place for literature in their lives? One of the most effective ways I have found is through the continuous monitoring of logs.

Determining where the readers are, what I should do next, and what support they need to further their learning and appreciation calls into play *assessment* strategies — the comments I make on ongoing student work as it progresses from early encounters with text through subsequent talking and writing, all a part of the learning process. Final products, on the other hand, come after the learning process and all the rehearsals and can include essays, projects, or a play performance, for example. Drawing on all that has gone before, these products are suitable for *evaluation*, resulting in a judgment about learning.

Assessment, like many things in life, is never linear. We may read before we write or talk, or we may talk before we read or write. Whether we are encountering a text for the first time or have had numerous experiences with it, tracking what happens to readers is essential.

On the pages that follow, I have outlined how I assess and evaluate students on three fronts: logs, contributions to group and class discussions, and final products. Generally, I allot marks as follows:

Log	50
Contributions to group, class discussions	20
Final product	30
Total	100

This allotment can be adjusted to reflect the nature of the unit. As an example, the drama unit entails a high degree of group work. In this instance, I change the structure of the marks so that contributions to group and class discussions constitute 50 percent of the mark, the reading response log, 30 percent, and the final product, 20 percent. For each of the chapters that follow, I outline the assessment and evaluation scheme, as well as instances where self-evaluation and peer evaluation can come into play.

A Teacher's Record Book

My record book is divided into two major sections. The first half comprises the tracking of ongoing learning assignments of each student; the second half comprises my personal log. A class list is accompanied by headings of assignments and my responses: checks, points, or blanks. The tracking process looks like this:

Title	LOG TO P.36	TO P.63	TO P.90	TO P.115	TO P.130	TO P.165	LOG	Drafting questions	Final Response	Discussion #1	Adam "web"	List of 3 Narrators	The "Real" Ending	Free Write Conclusion	Essay Draft
Appel, Maria	✓	✓	✓	✓	✓	✓	50	✓x	✓	✓	✓	✓	✓	✓	5
Chow, Anita		✓	✓		✓	✓	40		✓	✓	✓				✓	3
Doyle, Anthony	✓	✓	✓	✓	✓	✓	45	✓	✓	✓	✓	✓	✓	✓	5

The second half of the book looks like this:

Name: Eric Wo

Text: I Am the Cheese

Response: (1) Log: filled with questions throughout. At the end writes, " and this is what I think happened" and clearly sets out dream sequence.
(2) Participates fully in discussions. Keeps the group going. Uses questions from his log. Loves to argue and make a point.

I add summaries, observations, and notes to keep a measure of the pulse of the readers. Rather than spending time marking questions or paragraphs, I read the logs and respond by giving feedback or asking questions. I also listen in to small-group and whole-class discussions and note any observations in my record book. These reflections provide the substance of what I need for reporting purposes.

The Log: A Reader's Portfolio

The log is a natural portfolio. It traces reflections and responses throughout the reading experience and becomes the basis for discussions and conferences. It also contains a record of books read, pages read during independent reading time, scraps and mementos related to the readings — pictures, newspaper and magazine articles, and book and movie reviews. (I encourage students to be on the lookout for anything interesting in the newspapers that they come across that could be clipped and added to their log.) This is why a loose-leaf binder is the best vehicle for a log. Eventually it looks much like a scrapbook.

The log regularly includes opportunities for self-assessment and evaluation, invitations to be reflective and thoughtful about the processes of reading and responding, and contributions to and learning from the group. Sometimes, the students and I fill in the same checklist and compare our ideas in a conference.

Marking the Reading Response Logs

One thought struck me repeatedly as I read my first set of logs: I am peering into the minds of my readers. I can see what happens as they read and reread texts. Their writing tells me that they have read the text; provides me with information on their personal histories, perspectives, and experiences and how these factors interact with the text; and how they interpret what is happening in the text as they explain their responses first to themselves and then to their peers and me.

The first thing I do with the logs is to respond in the margins: "This is interesting," "I don't understand this," "What do you mean?" "Do you still think this is true?" "I've never seen it this way before." That leaves me with an overall impression of the log. I sometimes comment at the end of the log and make a suggestion: "In your small-group discussions, raise the issue of time frame in this novel," "It seems like that is a problem for you here," or a summary comment, "You amazed me with all those probing questions and then a clear discussion of the ending. I read the book three times before I understood that!"

What am I looking for when I assess student learning? How do I assess the work that the students are doing and mark it appropriately? First, I look for the level of engagement with the literature. How does the reader demonstrate involvement? A simple check as to whether or not all responses are complete will distinguish between a student working at a level of full commitment and one who has made a partial effort. Did the student bring his or her log to each class? For some students, such tracking and recording is necessary to help them realize that the logs are a serious component of their study.

Engagement with each topic is also demonstrated by the type of responses in the logs and their development as the reading progresses. In assessing a student's commitment to the work, his or her understanding of the literature, and his or her ability to make sense of the author's work, I use a three-stage rating scale. When enough assessments have been accumulated, I can make a judgment or evaluation on the stage a student has reached.

Stage 1. A literal surface encounter with the text
The work of students at this level will have some or many of these characteristics:

- an unreflective interest in the narrative,
- concerned primarily with retelling the text,
- superficial judgments unsupported by evidence from the text or from their own experience,
- predictions that are unrealistic or improbable given the unfolding scenario,
- inability to frame questions,
- inability to hypothesize,
- stereotypical responses,
- mental images drawn from television and movies,
- usually short and superficial entries,
- evidence of confusion or unresolved misunderstanding,
- off-topic responses.

Stage 2: Evidence of understanding and appreciation of text
The work of students at this level will have some or many of these characteristics:

- writing moves beyond a retelling of the narrative to a reflection,
- personal connections and comparisons are made between the text and the students' own experience,
- predictions are plausible given the scenario but are often short-term and relatively undeveloped,
- some ability to empathize with or understand the motivation of characters,
- some mention of other texts they are reminded of,
- ideas are sometimes unsophisticated and underdeveloped,
- some evidence that they are thinking about the text and working to understand it,
- ability to frame questions and to hypothesize and predict.

Stage 3. Synthesis and evaluation of the text
The work of students at this level will have some or many of these characteristics:

- a strong and active interest in the literature that shows awareness of levels of meaning,
- judgments are made based on the text and their own experience,
- predictions are sophisticated and demonstrate deep engagement with the text,
- expectations of the characters are consistent with the information in the text,
- show strong empathy with characters and understanding of decisions based on their own experience,
- comparisons and connections are found between the text and other literary and artistic works,
- recognition of the author's craft in making deliberate choices in composing the text that affect the way the reader feels and responds,
- recognition that writing is an imaginative construct,
- awareness that their own personal beliefs may be different from those expressed in the text,
- awareness of the writer's point of view.

Here are some typical statements made by students in response to the novel, *The Giver,* by Lois Lowry. In this novel, humans exist in a futuristic society in which their behavior is controlled and their emotions eliminated. Life is predictable and at first seems to be ideally comfortable. When twelve-year-old Jonas comes of age, he is told which of the many jobs he has been chosen for. He becomes "The Giver," the one member of the society who holds memories of the past.

STACEY: What is this release they keep on about? The elderly are released when they reach a certain age. I think this is much better than being forgotten and dying in a home. Everyone dresses the same here. And you have to tell your dreams so everyone can talk about them. Everyone is always watching you — there's no escape except when you're sleeping.

Most of her entries continue in the same vein. When she raises an interesting question, the issue of what is meant by "release," for example, she doesn't stop to ponder. Ideas surface but are never dealt with in any depth. I need to encourage her to stop, to wonder, to hypothesize, to make predictions, and to ask herself why characters do the things they do. I add a note to her in the margins, and characterize her initial responses as Level One.

JASON: I can already tell from the second page that this place is very controlled. There is lots of ritual and rules. Yet Jonas' family is very loving and caring. This seems like a contradiction. I don't think it would be all sweetness and light like this if my family were to be in this situation. I think about how my dad likes to tell us all what to think about something and everyone argues with him. We all like to voice our opinions in our family. I can't see us accepting this way of life.

The community doesn't seem quite so perfect now when they only let you have one boy and one girl per family. I wonder if children are taken away and assigned to the parents?

I was right. The family "received" Lily. So the birth mothers don't get to keep their own children. This seems cruel to me. Choice has been taken away from people.

Jason's engagement with the text approximates a Level Two response. Sometimes in his log he retells parts of the story to clarify it for himself. He wonders aloud and looks for the answers to his own questions. On occasion, he talks about times in his own experience that are recalled by reference to the text. He voices his opinions, and his log is a record of his gradual understanding of the main events and ideas in the story. Through written suggestions, I can try to push his thinking even further and have him consider some of the themes and issues that are raised in the novel in greater depth.

AMANDA: Sombre, sombre. A very dark feeling in the opening chapters. The tone reminds me of something I've seen — can't remember what but it had the same oppressive atmosphere. Something is missing. What is it? Can't put my finger on it yet. Perhaps it's real feelings. They seem too good to be true.

These people aren't real. Everything is bland. Maybe they are all drugged or something? Are they even alive? They could be robots who think they are really living. It's like 1984, everything is controlled and Big Brother is watching you. The role reversals are interesting though. The males are the nurturers and the females the law givers. What is the author saying here? That men should be more involved in looking after children? If so I agree, but I don't like the idea of releasing people at a certain time. Now what exactly does that mean — must watch out for further enlightenment!

Something I notice is that she doesn't really give us any physical descriptions. It's left up to us to visualize everything. The appearance of the people is left entirely (almost) up to the imagination. Perhaps that's because they all look alike? They certainly all behave alike. Come back to this later.

Amanda's responses meet criteria suggested for Level Three. She is puzzled by aspects of the story so makes notes to watch for patterns and solutions. She talks about how the book makes her feel and is reminded of other literary experiences she has had. Here is a student fully engaged with her reading, and who is using language to explore ideas and raise issues for further discussion. I hope that she will continue to write with such involvement throughout the course of the novel.

Reading aloud responses such as Amanda's can help other students to understand some of the characteristics of a thoughtful and articulate entry. As students move through a genre, I frequently give them several samples of responses to a text and ask them to rank them on a one (low) to three (high) scale. They also explain their reasons for the ranking.

As I note the ongoing responses, I ask students to reflect on their increase in the level of enjoyment and comprehension of the text, whether it be a short story, a novel, a poem, or a play. They reflect in their logs about their development as readers and set goals for growth, for example, "I will come to class with my log" or "I will try to imagine how characters felt in stories."

Of the 50 marks for the log, the majority are awarded for completion of and enthusiasm for the activities the student has undertaken. While the level of understanding that the student achieves contributes to the mark, I place strong emphasis on the daily reading and completion of entries because the *process* offers the greatest opportunity for learning.

Talking and Learning: How Can We Tell?

Keeping track of the ways that students discuss a text is no easy task for any teacher, inexperienced or experienced. In one "talk" workshop that comprised both student and experienced teachers, I surveyed the participants at the beginning of the session to see when and how they organized opportunities for talk in their classes. Differences between the groups were immediately apparent: student teachers worried about management issues while experienced teachers worried about the efficiency of talk given the extensive content of the course. One issue, however, was of utmost concern to both groups — how to keep students from straying off topic and off task.

Although I share this concern, I also realize that "all have sinned" when it comes to straying (workshops are excellent examples!). Douglas Barnes calls some of this "talk around the edges" and claims it can be a good thing since these forays sometimes provide the most interesting discussions.

Setting parameters for the discussion will help to contain the talk (e.g., "We will take twenty minutes to decide what the ending of the novel means. Scribble notes about your talk so you will be prepared for a whole-class discussion") and the consequences (e.g., "Report one question about the text from your discussion that your group could not answer. Be prepared to state how far you got in your discussions").

To track the learning that occurs during discussions, I begin by moving around the room in a random fashion and asking each group to "tell me" something about their discussion — the topic, the questions asked, and the insights the group has made. The second phase of tracking involves selecting one group for assessment. How involved is each member in the discussion? Does she or he contribute to the discussion? If yes, are his or her contributions meaningful? Is the discussion successful (i.e., does it further members' understanding and interest in the text at hand)?

I like to focus students' attention on ways in which they can become more active, sensitive, and thoughtful participants. As examples, I ask them to:

- share ideas and opinions openly,
- link their ideas to the ideas of others,
- support opinions with evidence, especially from the text,
- take turns to speak,
- offer ideas without dominating the discussion,
- invite others to contribute to the discussion,
- listen with interest to the ideas of others,
- give others credit for their ideas,
- be aware of time and topic,
- evaluate the work of the group.

Students can monitor their performance by completing a journal entry that includes responses to questions such as the following:

1. What did you do well in group discussion today?
2. What group-discussion skills do you need to work on?
3. What elements make for a productive small-group discussion?

Sometimes I request that students record one of their discussions and submit the tape. This assignment serves two purposes: it is useful for assessing the development of group-discussion skills, and it provides a window into the content of the discussions. I can determine if the students play an equal role, and if they are considerate of one another's point of view.

Everyone needs to become familiar with these aspects of small-group discussion and to take equal responsibility for them. For some people, learning to listen and refrain from dominating a discussion is difficult while others prefer to let more vocal members of the group assume responsibility for the talk. Time spent reflecting on the success of the small-group discussions is time well spent. The self-assessment checklist on the next page can help students to assess their performance in a group.

A PERSONAL CHECKLIST: ASSESSING GROUP WORK

After your group has met, complete this checklist to evaluate your contribution to the discussion.

Name: _____ Date: _____

Class: _____ Teacher: _____

As a member of the group, I	Yes	No	Sometimes
1. used my log for discussion			
2. shared my log with others			
3. knew what we were trying to accomplish			
4. stayed on task			
5. listened to others with interest			
6. allowed everyone to participate			
7. asked for clarification as needed			
8. encouraged others to speak			
9. added new information to my log			
10. supported my opinions with evidence from the text			

Of the final mark for the unit, students' contributions to group and class discussions is worth 20 percent. On some occasions, I base the mark on my observations of students' performance; at other times, I split the mark into two equal halves where half of the mark is based on my observations and the other half on student self-assessment using the above checklist.

Evaluation of Final Products

When students have finished reading, writing, and talking about a literature text, they are ready to generate a final response. These can come in a variety of forms — staging a scene from a play, writing a book review, a letter to an author, or an essay, or preparing for a debate. Final responses can be individual or shared, depending on the project and the interests of the students. Whatever form it takes, the final response grows out of the students' earlier experiences with the literature.

Preparation for this response will entail the use of the log and the recall of past discussions. Some students may scour their writing for "unfinished business" they want to work through while others will review their work and highlight related material they can use for a project. The process is much like assessment in that it requires reading, writing, and talking through a project. As well, it models the writing process: the response may begin with word lists, a set of questions, webs, diagrams, or freewrites before moving into stages of drafts, revisions, editing, and publishing. Regardless of the form chosen, the response is "performed." If a student writes a letter, she or he sends it; if a student writes a movie review, it is passed on to the local newspaper; if a student writes a children's story, it is read to a group of elementary students. Audience is vital to maintaining integrity and purpose for these projects.

Students document the entire process in a log. To help them, I set dates for each phase of the project and keep a record of their progress. Together, we decide what criteria will be used for evaluation. What grading system is most suitable? How will their response be judged? Who will judge their response — the teacher, themselves? peers? Typically, I allow 30 percent of the total mark for this project.

I get to know my students through a multitude of lenses. Through talk, reading, and writing we come to know each other and to develop a community of readers. From the outset, we are involved in creating criteria for the success of our learning during our time together, and actively engage in constructing an atmosphere in which learning can take place for everyone.

CHAPTER TWO

Exploring the Short Story

It was probably Ed who convinced me to start my English
classes with short stories. A member of a non-academic
Grade 12 class, Ed had a history of non-participation. On
the first day of the term, I found him lying on a bench.
Surprised, I gestured that he rise and move to a seat. Ed
did not budge. Finally, I suggested he find a seat. "This
is my place. I always lie here," he said. Others joined in,
"Yeah, he's been lying there since Grade 9!" "But how do
you write?" I asked. "I don't," he responded. "I haven't
written anything since Grade 9!" Given that Ed was large,
I thought it best to leave him.

Ed and his peers had made up their minds long ago that
school reading was not for them. It seemed pointless to
assign readings that I knew would not get read, so I
decided, from the first day, to read aloud to them. I chose
my stories with care, selecting only those I love to read
and hear, and that could be completed in one reading.
Students assumed the characteristic adolescent posture —
the slouch — and Ed remained on the bench. I had little
knowledge of where this might go, if anywhere, but I
trusted in the power of story.

After several stories, the students began to respond
furtively with a brief comment or remark. In time, their
discussions became more spontaneous. They began to talk
as readers: what made a story "good" or "so-so," what the
story reminded them of, and what they thought of the
story's outcome. I began reading stories that were too long
to finish in one class, always stopping them at a particularly tense or poignant moment. Students left class talking
about the story and came back anxious to hear the rest.
After six weeks, Ed sat up to the amazement of his peers
and gradually became an active participant in class.

Selecting Stories for Reading Aloud

Good short stories can bring us a long way in offering "assisted invitations" into the world of reading. They come in a grand array of textures, flavors, shapes, and sizes. The stories I select for reading aloud are usually my favorites. I also consider (in no particular order):

- the group of students and their previous reading experiences,
- the length of a story,
- oral possibilities (e.g., dialect, rich in pregnant pauses),
- a strong plot line,
- a surprise ending,
- suspense and high drama,
- a story students might not select for themselves,
- a range of story types,
- a story that deals with familiar adolescent problems,
- a story's overall appeal to students.

My repertoire for read-aloud stories grew as my experience with them evolved. I added new stories and deleted others, all the while keeping in mind that story availability, in either a school or library anthology, is a major factor. The following list includes some of the most successful read-aloud stories I have used with readers of all ages.

"An Occurrence at Owl Creek Bridge" by Ambrose Bierce
A man is hanged on a bridge for deserting the army, and lives to tell about it.

"Henry" by Phyllis Bottome
Henry is a lion whose trainer takes him just one step too far in the ring.

"The Weapon" by Frederic Brown
The mentally challenged son of a scientist working on an atomic bomb finds a gun.

"The Most Dangerous Game" by Richard Connell
The hunter is the hunted in this story of suspense where the most dangerous game to play is one in which the loser looses life itself.

"Poison" by Roald Dahl
A man comes home to find his friend motionless in bed because a highly poisonous snake is also in the bed.

"The Dinner Party" by Mona Gardner
A snake hidden under a dinner table tests a woman's bravery.

"Thank You, Ma'am" by Langston Hughes
An intended victim of a thief turns the tables by marching the boy to her home where she makes him wash his face and then feeds him a meal.

"Uneasy Homecoming" by Will Jenkins
Returning from a two-week holiday to an empty house, Connie becomes increasingly nervous. The suspense builds as she realizes a murderer is in the house and she knows his identity.

"Mrs. Adis" by Sheila Kaye-Smith
Mrs. Adis hides a wild animal poacher in her house while the police search for him.

"Leiningen Versus the Ants" by Carl Stephenson
A Brazilian plantation owner is threatened by an incredible ten-mile long column of fierce ants that is marching toward his plantation and eating everything in its path. He must flee or prepare his defences.

Over time, many of us will have read these stories to any number of students so it is difficult to remember our first reading and initial reaction. The students, through discussion and written reflections, can remind us of the experience of coming to this story for the first time.

I love to read aloud, and have learned to use my voice to my advantage by reading slowly, softly, hesitantly, or rapidly, and pausing at moments where the tension in the story leaves listeners on the edge of their seats. This style of reading takes practice but it is well worth the effort. Preparation means finding the right story and reading it aloud, perhaps on tape, until I get the feel of it. I note the time the oral reading takes and make marginal notes such as "slowly," "stop/pause," or "step up pace." Sometimes it is useful to note stopping points where students can predict, ask questions, offer advice to a character, or note new observations about the narrative, either through a brief discussion or notes in their log.

One of the first factors that emerges from these initial experiences is a realization that all responses, particularly those first, tentative responses, are valid. Students' initial responses must be treated with respect if we want them to grow in their ability to enjoy and understand short stories and become members of a genuine community of thoughtful readers. As Aidan Chambers (1993) says, "In helping children talk well about their reading it is essential, for children and adults alike, to agree that everything is honourably reportable." All must engage, then, in respectful listening and all must trust that the other members of the community will accept their ideas seriously. The kind of invitation extended into the world of short stories affects how readers respond and come to grow in understanding and appreciating the genre. The sort of short stories we choose will challenge readers, stimulate discussion, and prompt further reading. These events can only happen if we create a classroom climate in which "everything is honourably reportable."

Defining the Short Story

Before Ed and his peers were willing to talk and think about stories, they had the opportunity to hear a number of them read aloud. In other classes, I have read two or three stories and then asked students to think about the short story. What is a short story? What is a short story "made of?" What are the who, what, where, and how of short stories?

Creating a web of components and characteristics of a short story often serves as a strong introduction to the study of this genre. This activity, which is most successful when students work with a partner, has them construct a visual representation of the short story as they understand it. To help them start their webs, I suggest that they begin by:

• talking about all the short stories they have heard or read,
• listing, in their logs, characteristics each story shares.

Students are then asked to:

• say aloud words or phrases,
• write these words and phrases in their log,
• group all related words and phrases,
• continue saying and writing words until they have recorded everything they know about the genre,
• record the grouped words and phrases in a web (students with limited experience in creating webs may find a model helpful).

In this way, an environment is created where each student thinks about and contributes to the discussion of the short story with his or her partner. Together, they assemble their information and present it to the whole group. Since each student has used his or her log to work through the process, everyone has a record of responses. As Tammy (and a host of theorists) state, "You can't write without thinking!" To have all readers thinking during the process is an event not to be underestimated. Pairing the students takes the pressure off individuals and demonstrates clearly the advantages of "two heads are better than one," particularly if this process is new to them.

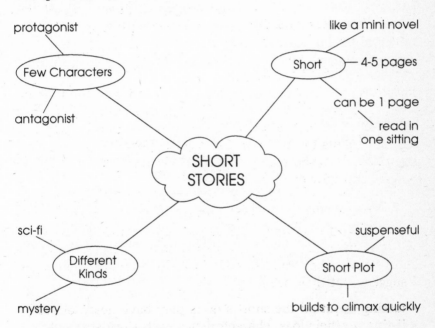

When all pairs of students have completed their work, the whole class gathers to create a class web on chart paper. It is sometimes useful to begin by listing the major categories for the web, for example, characters, setting, theme, and plot. Each pair of students then adds information to one of the categories listed on the chart.

A class web provides students with more components to add to their personal webs they recorded earlier in their logs, and is a good visual reference for the remaining short story experiences. As the readings progress, additional information can be added to both class and personal webs.

Captivating readers with a story can have dramatic effects. Recently I read the wonderful short story "Thank You, Ma'am" by Langston Hughes to a group of Grade 10 students. In this story, a boy attempts to steal a woman's purse. The woman catches him, and marches him to her apartment where she makes him wash his face and feeds him a meal. Finally, the woman gives the boy money and sends him on his way.

Students listened intently to the entire story and then recorded their responses in a 10-minute freewrite. To help them begin, I asked them to describe how they felt about the story, and what part or character struck them the most. Students were made aware of the fact that their responses would be shared with the whole class at the end of the freewriting period.

The following extracts from the logs show the range of student responses and the sort of thinking that occurs when students are given an open-ended task.

TANYA: A very interesting story. I found the characters quite plausible and the way the story was introduced, with a description, though common, was captivating. (general response)

JEN: I enjoyed the story because I thought it had a lot of meaning and made me think. (personal response)

ELINA: I loved the woman. I would hug her. (personal response)

JEN: Mrs. Louella Bates Washington Jones is a perfect name. It is a name that has connotations of a proper, stately woman with fussy, curly hair and a good, well-made pair of leather brown shoes with thick wedge heels. (character)

WILLIAM: The woman had knowledge about people. She didn't MAKE him feel guilty. She made him make himself feel guilty. (character)

VERNA: The boy's conscience is something not often found. The way that the lady made the boy feel guilty without doing anything. I don't like the woman's character. (character)

TANYA: The plot was perfect. Straight into the story with a captivating intro, into a story of this large woman lecturing a boy who had just attempted to rob her; into a climax (ending) that closes things perfectly. (plot)

PRISCILLA: I liked how the author "showed" the characters instead of telling us about them. It seemed like I was there, watching everything happen. It seemed very real, how the boy was snatching the woman's purse. (character)

Other responses began to reflect the theme of the story, taking a wider view.

SHANNON: It was very enjoyable to hear of how a woman who was not so well off herself, could be so kind to a common thief. Although the boy was not quite common. Perhaps she herself had thieved when she was his age and that's why she felt it necessary to teach him right from wrong.

Jason and Verna both related the story to their own experience.

JASON: I got the impression she ran a group home or something.

VERNA: I feel as though this could not have happened in a time like today because it is difficult to find anyone trusting enough to take in a potential thief to "wash their face."

At the end of the freewrite, students reread their responses. It was time to put the logs into a second dimension as a "text for talk." Having written responses, students were ready to discuss their first encounters with the story. Their talk at this stage was animated — they had time to reflect on the story and now had an opportunity to discuss their thoughts and read them aloud from their logs. Here is a sample of one discussion.

PRISCILLA: Here are things I liked: the characters seemed motivated; the author showed the characters really well; the idea was good — I mean it wasn't violent like T.V. The story was simple — even I understood it (laughter) yeah 'cos I don't get things sometimes but the details were good and it ended quickly.

JOHN: Yeah, I thought the ending was effective. It was quite humorous and I wondered maybe she was kind of lonely.

JEN: Lonely, I'm kind of like that and the boy probably was too. I wondered what did she have in her pocketbook and who would want blue-suede shoes anyway?

WILLIAM: It was the 50's wasn't it?

VERNA: Yeah I couldn't see it happening today. I couldn't imagine the face washing. But I thought perhaps she had it happen to her you know.

PRISCILLA: Yeah, that's why she took him in to teach him a lesson.

JEN: I still think she was lonely. I can just imagine her with her shoes — purposeful — she knows where she needs to be, sort of zen navigation!

These responses, while unstructured and spontaneous, appear to validate the use of a response-based approach to literature. Students were obviously engaged and interested in the story. They enjoyed the experience and that enjoyment is heard in their voices. Although they did not analyze the story in the traditional way, their discussion dealt with aspects of character, plot, setting, and theme. Their personal views were respected and differences of opinion aired. Ownership of the literature rests with the readers, and not with an external expert who has told them what to think.

Interrupted Readings

Sometimes, as I read a story, I will pause at several points so that the students can reflect on what they have heard and consider how their responses change as the story progresses. This alerts them to the possibility of diverse responses as the story evolves. On occasion, students will talk about what they have heard. More often, they will write a short response to the story before I resume reading. While these pauses may be trying to readers who want to know the outcome of the story, I support Russ Hunt (1982) in his belief that slowing the process by thinking and writing is a necessary component of understanding literature. When one pauses to think about what has been heard or read, the time allows for identification and expression of one's ideas.

A class of Grade 10 students recently worked with "The Case for the Defense" by Graham Greene. The story concerns the trial of a man accused of a brutal murder. As witnesses testify against the defendant, who claims to have been with his wife at the time of the murder, his twin brother arrives in court. He too has an alibi. Unable to find the first brother guilty, he is acquitted. As the two brothers leave the courtroom, one brother is pushed in front of a bus and killed. The story has an ambiguous ending and leaves many unanswered questions. Unlike "Thank You, Ma'am," this story was read with pauses situated at specific points through the story. Students began their work with the story by writing about what the title suggested to them. Answers included:

MYRNA: A bad lawyer story.
GARY: A football story with a bad defensive quarterback.
ANDREW: Bad generic character that gets caught.

ASHLEIGH: I really don't expect a lawyer story — that would be too obvious. Something a little more subtle, like a metaphor or a hidden meaning/message.

ANDREA: One would expect a lawyer story. Yes. What else, with a name like this? FOOLS! Of course it's not a law story.

After listening to the first two paragraphs, students wrote a response to what they had heard and any questions they had about the story to that point.

KENT: I'm lost. Has there been a murder?

ANDREW: Was there a murder committed? Where?

MYRNA: It's a flashback. We're back at the murder scene.

At this point, students were confused. Events of the story were unclear and left them in a state of suspense.

Continuing with the story, students heard the evidence of the prosecution witnesses. Pausing at these words, "It was all over, you would have said but the hanging," I asked students if they agreed or disagreed with this statement. Here are some sample answers.

MYRNA: Adams is being found guilty or at least that's what the crown is expecting to happen.

KENT: I think there is something missing that we haven't been told yet. If this is all there is to the story, it's pretty bad. He can't be guilty, or what's the point?

ANDREA: He's not guilty. He's got something that he's hiding in the background. HE'S NOT GUILTY!!

The third pause in the telling of the story came after the introduction of the twin brother. There was still some uncertainty about what was happening: students could draw no firm conclusions at this point.

GARY: Twin brother! Can't convict either. Who knows which it really was? Talk about reasonable doubt!

MYRNA: One of the twins is covering up for the other and the innocent one comes forward.

ASHLEIGH: Did I miss something? Was one guy already arrested? Suppose the guy was guilty? Why would the twin show up to court?

KENT: Identical twins tend to be very attached. Perhaps they both did it.

At the story's conclusion, students wrote their general response to the story.

ANDREA: I LOVE this story. Each of my predictions were either wrong or had a twist to it. I love stories that are not predictable. The guilty one survived.

ASHLEIGH: I'm not sure what to make of this story. Great suspense, that's for sure. There are so many loose ends in this story. It's really hard to follow along.

KENT: Aaarrrgh! Incredible story. So many twists you trip over them. Adams and Adams are pretty strange. The question, of course, is "Why?" Why kill Mrs. Parker? Why didn't the lawyer know about the twin? And who pushed Adams in front of the bus?

Assessment and Evaluation Criteria for the Short Story Unit

Before students engage in independent work, I like to discuss with them my expectations for their learning. For this unit, these expectations typically include:

- engaging with the short stories and demonstrating involvement with the story at hand,
- completing assigned responses,
- bringing their logs to each class,
- growing in their level of response and thinking,
- understanding components of the short story,
- identifying and defining characteristics of a short story (e.g., structure, theme, characterization, plot development),
- recognizing the range and variety of the genre,
- choosing to read short stories in personal time,
- contributing to small-group discussions.

As suggested on page 22, logs will account for 50 marks; contributions to group and class discussions, 20; and the final product, 30. Knowing the criteria before they begin their independent work helps students to identify their responsibility for learning and alerts them to the fact that assessment and evaluation are not reserved solely for an end-of-unit project.

Further Encounters and Explorations

After listening to several stories read aloud, with and without pauses, students are ready to begin their independent reading. Two strategies, outlined here, help students to monitor their work with short stories.

• Ranking the Stories
After reading four or five stories, students record the titles and rank them from 1 (low) to 5 (high). They then form small groups of three where they are asked to explain their ranking and compare findings with their peers. This activity usually results in a lively discussion as students defend their choices and as a consequence their literary tastes. Keeping a list of each group's rankings throughout the duration of the short story unit provides evidence of the amount students have read and the diverse range of responses a story can elicit.

• Adding to the Short Story Web
Students can check their original short story webs with a partner (see page 36) in order to elaborate on previously recorded information. They may know more about how characters are presented ("shown," as Priscilla said earlier), plot lines, style, personal responses, and/or themes. Each set of partners can contribute additional items to the class web. The intent is to continue to add to the web throughout the duration of work with the story. The end result will form a strong statement of students' learning.

Through the years, the most successful pattern I have found for independent reading is structured on the three Rs — readin', 'riting, and rappin'. In this mode, students read a short story and write their responses to it as they read and after they have finished the story. They then use their logs to talk with a partner or as a part of a small group. This allows all students to prepare for a discussion that involves the whole community of readers.

Why is discussion so important? I had been experimenting with logs for some time and believed strongly in the power of response through writing — our students were living testimony to that. In time, however, I began to develop a growing sense that the picture was incomplete. The constrained audience for the log (the teacher) as well as the highly personal nature of much of the writing did not satisfy me or the readers. What they needed was to spend time sharing responses with others. Since all readers come to texts in unique ways, why not share the wealth? Why not see all class members as active participants and contributors to the development of responses in the community? I made the decision that the logs would become not only personal explorations for the readers but also text for talk with a wider audience — their peers. When instituted, the change was immediately obvious — students wanted and needed time to talk.

I asked students to reflect on what the process meant to them. "The discussions were fun and made you think again about your quick judgments" wrote Tanya. Kent commented, "The discussions were a big part for me in understanding the stories. I loved the discussion and making my opinion known. I also learned more through the discussion."

Moving to Independent Reading

How do the students select the stories they will read? There are several strategies that are quite successful, and which add to the students' ability to think beyond the surface of the words.

1. To predict from titles, select 10 stories and pass them around to the students. Ask them to read the title, write a comment about it, and assign a ranking from 1 (low) to 10 (high) that indicates their interest in reading the story. When they have completed this process for the titles, students can select the five highest-ranking stories for their independent reading. An extension of this is to have them rank the 10 titles and give reasons for their views. Record the class preferences on a chart or blackboard. Which title is most popular? least popular? Why?

2. To predict from summaries, provide the class with brief summaries of the 10 stories. After students have read the summaries, ask them to reconsider their initial ranking. Does reading the summaries change their minds about which stories they think will be most interesting? A small-group discussion on shifts in opinion draws students' attention to how their life experiences combined with additional information — the summaries — often results in the revision of opinions.

3. Predicting from introductions is an alternative way for students to form a sense of a story. Short stories, by their very nature,

waste little time in introducing characters, setting, and plot. Readers are quickly transported into the world of the narrative as Tanya so aptly said, "straight into the story with a captivating introduction."

Examining introductions and deciding how effectively they "set the stage" draws attention to the tools of the writer's trade and develops a growing awareness in our readers. Generally, they sense what draws or repels them but are often unable to explain why. This strategy helps them not only in their reading (writerly reading), but also in their writing (readerly writing). Introductions present a multitude of ways into a short story.

If possible, provide students with one- or two-paragraph introductions to the stories. After they have read an introduction, they can record their thoughts in their logs on what they have read and what they think the story will be about. The words or phrases they use to capture their thoughts can be written as a list, a web, or a diagram, or as a freewritten response.

When students have discussed each introduction with a partner, they can assemble as a group to share their perceptions of the introductions. Each group presents one finding about the introductions and others add to it. As each group reports, members of the class can add any additional items to their logs.

It's always interesting to see how students rate potential stories. After each discussion, ask the students to rate the introduction. What makes for an excellent introduction? a mediocre introduction? a weak introduction? What might these authors have done to better captivate potential readers? Such discussions keep readers focussed on the writing and make them aware of the tools they need to employ in their own writing.

Independent Reading: From Selecting Through Sharing

Students are now ready to pick a number of stories to read. Five is usually a good number as it provides students with sufficient latitude for choice. No doubt, there will be evidence of a diversity of tastes. Most often, the preference for stories has a rather even distribution although choice of stories can vary greatly from class to class. I once read a set of introductions to three Grade 9 English classes; each class chose a different "favorite!"

Students jot down the titles of the stories they are about to read in their logs. To help you monitor choice, consider labeling the title of each story on a piece of chart paper. As well as listing their choices in their logs, students can sign up for the stories they will read, identifying the first story with a "1," the second with a "2," and so on. A "status-of-the-class" check will alert you and the students to the stories selected; students who have selected the same first story to read will form a group. For each story selected, students will form new groups as it is unlikely that members of any one group will have selected all of the same stories.

To begin, students note the title and the author of the story. If they wish, they can reflect on the title before they begin. As the students read, they use their logs to document their reactions and questions to the story. They can also record whether they felt they made a good choice in selecting this story, whether it developed as they thought it would, and finally whether they think the author was successful in his or her efforts. Remind students to date and number their entries. Page numbers should be recorded for those entries that refer to a specific passage. Log entries can consist of:

- freewritten responses,
- a list of questions and answers,
- diagrams,
- a plot line,
- character webs,
- a Venn diagram,
- evaluations of the story.

Once all members of a group have finished the story, they meet to discuss their views and reactions using the logs as a basis for the discussion. Having students exchange logs so that they can read another's entries helps to further the discussion since they can share opinion in two ways — through reading and through talk. What did each member make of the story? Did it fulfill his or her initial expectations? Can the members come to a consensus regarding the story? Have the students take five minutes at the end of the discussion to record in their logs what they noticed about other members' reactions and opinions, what they learned from the discussion, and how talking about the story changed — or didn't change — their thinking.

Students then form jigsaw groups where each member has read a different story. They take turns telling others in the group about the story they read, including their reactions, what it meant to them, and whether they would recommend it to others. When finished, members can reassemble for a group share that results in a ranking of the stories and brief comments on each. A class list of preferences can evolve from these sessions.

If you notice a group having difficulty, you can spur their conversation by asking them to tell you about their discussion. You may hear a facet of their retelling that requires further exploration or that leads to a point that has yet to be addressed. You can also share your own responses to the story if you think the members might benefit from added input. The time spent with groups allows you to record the progress of individuals as they work and note substantive comments on the spot.

Developing Categories of Short Stories

By now students have heard, read, written about, and discussed short stories that vary in style, content, and effect. As well, they have had an opportunity to rank the stories and contribute to a class list. Students are now ready to categorize the short stories and create a grid (see below). This activity is best done in small groups of four or five members.

The first step groups will take will be to consider basic ways stories can be categorized. One example is to group them by genre, for example, action, moral, real life, imaginative, suspenseful, or humorous. Categories can be numbered and the stories given corresponding numbers. One story may fit three categories; others only one. One of the most effective ways of showing categories is to place story characteristics on the horizontal axis of a matrix and story titles on the vertical axis, like this:

Story Title	clever character	surprise ending	nature important	setting
Lenigen versus the Ants				
Mrs. Adis				

Each group presents their matrix to the other groups, later posting it on the wall. After each presentation, students can ask questions, challenge a category, or add stories to other categories.

Students can go back to the original short story web they constructed in their logs to refine their creations. They think about stories in general and about some stories in particular. How are stories put together? What elements characterize them? The next page shows how one group of Grade 10 students added to their class web the "second time around."

Sharing Favorite Short Stories

All of us have favorite short stories. Acknowledging our students' favorites reinforces the validity of each community member's response. Enthusiasm for a favorite story, however, is often infectious. How often have we, as experienced adult readers, been led to a great story by someone's recommendation? Each reader brings different experiences to a reading. As a result, we judge a story as "great" for different reasons. Jotting brief notes in their logs about their favourite story helps students keep the information up front and brings the selection process to the foreground. Why select this story? What is it that makes it stand out from the rest? Why would anyone else want to read this story?

A fun activity for the students is to ask them to meet as a whole class to form a short story club. Each student brings a favorite story and has two minutes to tell others about its merits and entice them to read it. This can result in the creation of a list of favorite short stories that can be posted on the wall. The short story "Genie Awards" can be given for the:

- most unforgettable character,
- most drama and suspense,
- best all-round story,
- most interesting setting,
- best plot line,
- best potential movie,
- most imaginative,
- most realistic,
- most powerful theme,
- most entertaining.

These "awards" can be debated in a class discussion. The top three stories from each category can then be awarded by a committee. This keeps the stories in the minds of the students and helps them "rehearse" their developing understanding.

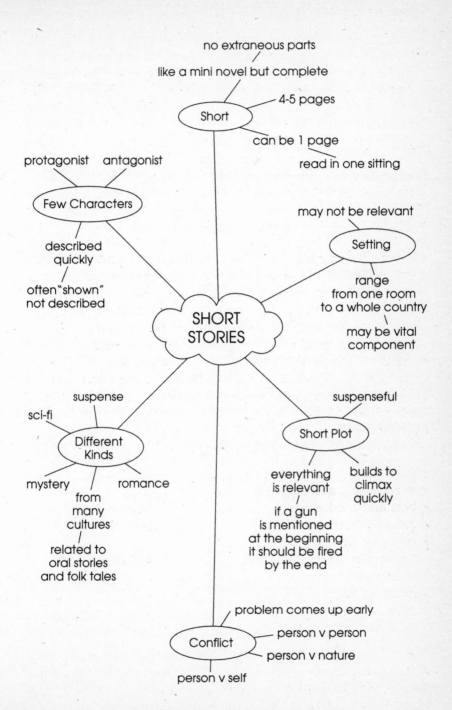

no extraneous parts

like a mini novel but complete

Short

4-5 pages

can be 1 page

read in one sitting

protagonist   antagonist

Few Characters

described
quickly

often "shown"
not described

Setting

may not be relevant

range
from one room
to a whole country

may be vital
component

SHORT
STORIES

suspense

sci-fi

Different
Kinds

mystery   romance

from
many
cultures

related to
oral stories
and folk tales

suspenseful

Short Plot

everything
is relevant

builds to
climax
quickly

if a gun
is mentioned
at the beginning
it should be fired
by the end

Conflict

problem comes up early

person v person

person v nature

person v self

Bringing It All Together: Evaluation Activities

At the end of the unit, students need to complete an activity that demonstrates their learning. Products of the following activities will reveal their understandings of the genre. All activities, which require that the students work individually, are suitable for evaluation and will account for 30 percent of the final mark for the unit.

When they have completed their activities, students can assemble in small groups to compare their reflections on the short story unit. They can ask one another questions, make suggestions, elaborate, argue, or respond to one another using their logs. This last option adds a new dimension to response that includes a written dialogue between two readers in the community.

1. Create a web that documents two of the most interesting characters from the same or different short stories.
2. Create a Venn diagram of two short stories or elements from the stories.
3. Write a new ending for a short story.
4. Write a "meanwhile, back at the ranch" episode about a short story character who is "off-stage" from the action.
5. Write, in role, a set of letters between two characters that explains their predicaments and tells about their lives.
6. Change the setting to determine its influence on a story's development.
7. Script an interview with a short story character — the interview should focus on a pivotal event in his or her life.
8. Rewrite a story from a minor character's point of view and note how it changes the story.

CHAPTER THREE

Invitations Into the Novel

Ed had much to teach me about literature and good
teaching. During the reading of *Cry, the Beloved Country*,
he found himself deeply and personally involved in the
narrative world. He filled fourteen pages with his
responses, which included questions, discoveries,
observations, and reactions. This is an example from
his log.

> *"I've been looking at this book all wrong. I was thinking it was
> about Umfundisi and his family. And the country was just the
> setting. But now I feel it's about the country and he just uses
> Umfundisi and his family to show what the country is like. I've
> been looking at it all wrong. Obviously, the title is "Cry, the
> beloved country."*

After reading Ed's log, I could hardly wait to talk to him
about it. I found him during a class change. "Ed," I said,
"I've just finished reading your responses. I was deeply
touched by your insights. I learned things that I certainly
had not thought of in my reading, and I felt as though you
were describing your reading experience to me!" Never
will I will forget Ed's response. He took the log, hugged it
to his chest, and beamed at me. All this for a young man
who only months earlier had lain on a bench and proudly
announced he had not "written anything since Grade 9!"
What had made the difference? He had been treated as an
equal partner in the reading experience, his thoughts and
feelings valued and respected. The log had provided him
with a place to talk and by using it, Ed had discovered that
reading can be a powerful experience.

A Changing of the Guard

Like short stories, novels come in a vast array of styles, types,
and sizes, as do the response strategies that accompany them.
The principle of responding to the literature, however, remains
the same. Students' ideas and responses should be the starting

point for study. Research tells us that this is not the case in the majority of high school classrooms, where students are asked on average about 100 questions per lesson. This amounts to a daunting 50,000 questions per school year. These questions often bear little resemblance to the questions students would ask — many require set answers and are designed to allow students to display their knowledge or understanding of what the teacher has taught.

In a response-based classroom, questions are authentic and are often asked by the students. Learning involves active inquiry. We learn when we ask questions, formulate a tentative hypothesis, and seek data to confirm or disprove our predictions. Through the use of reading response logs, students learn to interrogate the text to seek the meaning it holds for them.

Using a log to explore literature gives ownership to the reader, involves him or her in understanding the text as a deliberate and conscious activity, and brings life and substance to literary discussions in the classroom. If I needed more validation for the process, I would have to look no further than the reflections of students who have engaged in novel study using logs. Here is a transcript of a tape-recorded conversation between Leslie, Cory, and Tammy as they discuss their experiences with logs.

LESLIE: The reason I liked it is, I have something in my mind and I forget it by the time I finish reading the book, then my questions are still there, but I don't remember what they are, so I don't know the book that well. I just sort of read, "Oh well, I'll come to this later. Maybe it'll answer it" and it doesn't and then I don't really care to ask anybody because I've finished the book so there's no point.

CORY: Yeah, yeah.

LESLIE: That's why I liked those log things because I can answer my own questions because I know what they are.

CORY: I found it almost made you have to learn the story, because, because you're always reading over your notes, which just gave you, you just kept on reading them over and trying to find something, and by the end, I had a really good grasp of what the story was about and the characters.

TAMMY: And you had to concentrate more. And because you're concentrating, you're learning. Because you couldn't, there's no way you could write anything down, if you're not concentrating. And also, you have to analyze it all the way through. Not just the characters, not just the action, all of it.

These comments reflect the potential benefits of thoughtful and purposeful talk about literature. Students profit from discussion when they have a stake in it, are free to express themselves, and can think through issues as they speak. They contribute their understanding to the group and benefit from the contributions of others. In a small group — a safe environment for most students — they can ask questions, modify their understanding, and challenge others in the quest to increase their understanding.

Invitations into the Novel: A Whole-Class Experience

The first paragraph of *Smith*, by Leon Garfield, introduces its readers to a twelve-year-old orphan who survives by picking people's pockets. The story is set in eighteenth-century London, a city marked by smallpox and consumption, among other things, all of which Smith has avoided. He is a speedy thief whose victims are aware only of "the powerful whiff of his passing and a cold draft in their dexterously emptied pockets."

When I have finished reading aloud the first paragraph, I ask students: "What do you know about Smith?" "Who is this Smith person?" "Where is he?" "What does he do?" "How does he operate?" "When do you think his story takes place?" I then ask them to think about the picture they have of Smith in their mind and write everything they have learned about him in their log as quickly as possible. Here are some examples:

JOHN: Smith - a very skilled pickpocket
- very devious
- twelve years old
- nothing could catch him
- lives in St. Pauls, dumpy sort of town
- smells bad
- long time ago

JENNIFER: Brief, fast. Passion for danger — spirit of challenging, cunning child. Powerful whiff of his passing — street urchin-smelly. Picture of little tramp lifting people's watches in olden days (Dickens) city.

When students have finished, they team up with a partner to compare and add to the notes in their log. Through discussion, they remember more details, identify what they think is the most important information, and clarify their understandings. John wrote, "I thought St. Pauls was the name of a town. His 'dumpy sort of town' was a reference to the 'tumble-down mazes about fat St. Pauls.'" John's partner Tanya wrote, "Smith is swift, fast, mysterious, a thief, curious, in a small 'Huck Finn town.'" When she discusses her writing with John, she notes that her assumption about the town was based on the words "tumble-down." Together, they decide that the town is clearly the bustling metropolis of London and St. Pauls is a cathedral. They are not certain of the time, and so for now "the olden days" will have to suffice. After students have had a few minutes to discuss their writing with a partner, I ask them to gather as a class. Each set of partners contributes something they have learned about Smith to a class chart. The chart, as will be shown, is intended to "grow as we go."

Smith is:

- an urchin
- swift, nimble, fleet of foot
- probably quite small
- a pickpocket
- like Gavroche in the musical "Les Miserables"
- in London, England
- in the olden days
- smelly
- elusive
- legendary
- afraid of the hangman
- image of evil? Does he enjoy it like in *Clockwork Orange*?

After reviewing the list, it seems to students that Smith's life is a bleak one. I ask them to predict what they think will happen to him, based on what has been read. In pairs, students begin to generate an outline of Smith's life as they predict it. As a class, we hear what others project and compare. I record their predictions on a chart that is posted for future reference.

VERNA: He will be approached by some people (bad people) and will get into trouble.

JOEL: He will get caught but will get reformed and find a family; there'll be a happy ending.

JOHN: The kid will get caught and sent to an orphanage from which he escapes.

Before we resume reading, I pose the following scenario to them: "If Smith — dirty, smelly and runty — would grace our room now by walking in that door, what would you ask him? What do you want him to tell you about himself? Record in your log as many questions as you can draft in the next few minutes." They come up with all kinds of questions for Smith:

> *Who are you?   What's it like to live on the streets?*
> *What do you want?   Why do you do what you do?   Do you enjoy life?*
> *Do you think you are going to die?   Do you care?*
> *Where are your parents?   What made you afraid of the hangman?*
> *Who taught you to pick pockets so well?*

Later, in reading their logs, I find the irreverent thinking of typical sixteen-year-olds. Questions for Smith include: "How did you get here?" "Aren't you dead?" "What do you think of Tanya's hair?" "How did you skip into this time frame?" "Don't you hate it when people tell you to chill?" as well as comments such as "Stay away from my pockets!" and "Phew, what's that smell?" The notion that we might actually bring Smith to life and have him walk into the room obviously intrigued them. As a teacher, I had used it as a device to have them think about the character. Students, on the other hand, obviously took the question literally.

I ask the students to call out their questions so I can record them on a chart. On occasion, I will ask students to group them into categories (e.g., childhood, problems, pick-pocket trade). The main point of posting the questions is to track how many are answered as the novel unfolds. Throughout the reading, students can check predictions, answer questions that were posed earlier, and feed their growing knowledge of Smith. This is an important aspect of a response-based program since taking ownership of a text through the expression of predictions, questions, and evolving knowledge keeps a reader focused and attentive. The end result of such a process is readers who act as interactive partners with the book and with one another.

The reading of *Smith* now begins in earnest. When I have only one copy of a book that is worth sharing, I read it all (there are limits — no Dostoevsky in spite of its literary value!). When I have sufficient copies to give to the students, I may start the process by reading aloud until they are thoroughly "hooked." Students then read individually according to stages of reading and responding that I set with them. Regardless of how the story is read, students respond in their logs and talk about their responses on a daily basis.

Some may wonder at the choice of having all students read and respond to the same novel, despite the variety of readers, tastes, and experiences any class will hold. After much experimentation, I've learned that class novels are fundamental to building a community of readers, a crucial component of any response-based class. Reading a class novel is a shared experience that generates a common bond so necessary for literary discussions. Students share the same points of reference and experience the response process together, learning as they go that we do not all think and feel alike when responding to literature. They need to learn how to ask questions of the text and how to respect the opinions of others in discussion. As the class novel may be too difficult for some to read unaided, discussions and chapters read aloud will be of benefit to them. Others may find the novel a fast-paced read and finish quickly. These students have the time to write more and in more depth. They also have the opportunity to read another novel by the same author. Leon Garfield's *Jack Diamond*, *The Sound of Coaches*, or *The Apprentices* may be compared with *Smith*. The amount of reading and writing that each student can be expected to do must be tailored to his or her learning needs in destreamed classes. In graded classrooms, set texts may well dictate what is to be studied by all; the differences among readers will be reflected in the way they meet the expectations set for the response-based activities.

For the first experience with a class novel, it is often effective to focus on particular ways of responding. *Smith*, for instance, invites predictions. Like Dickens, Garfield drops little "bombs" or unexpected twists at the end of each chapter. As an example, the end of the first chapter finds our hero stealing a document from an unsuspecting man who is then murdered by two men dressed in brown. Smith watches as the two conduct what is obviously a fruitless search for something on the victim's person. When the two men spot Smith, they give chase believing correctly that he has what they are looking for. Smith escapes them and when safe, sits down with his loot — the document. Smith now faces a major obstacle for he is illiterate.

The end of Chapter One invites a response. What will Smith do? Where will he go? How will he uncover the contents of the document? Who can help him? What advice would you give Smith? What's in the document?

As students write their responses to the chapter's conclusion, I also write having learned the power of modeling and the importance of being a genuine member of the reading community. When I first initiated this strategy, students who wrote rarely, if at all, watched me read and write before shrugging their shoulders and doing the same! Here are sample end-of-chapter responses.

VERNA: He's going to try to find one of his friends to help him read the note. He will make sure he knows where it is at all times and be careful not to see those men again.

JENNIFER: He'll turn to someone — an older thief — a mentor, teacher-like figure and ask for assistance; no going to the police, obviously because he'd get caught for thieving and removing evidence from a scene.

TANYA: – throw away the document; try to get someone he trusts to read it; try to sell it or trade it to the murderers.

Students reach consensus about two things — we have not heard the last of the men in brown, and Smith will keep the document. Response remains central to the reading experience, with students writing about characters and events, forming questions, making predictions, and creating timelines, webs, diagrams, sketches, and maps. Each mode of response, which is used as text for talk, allows for an evolvement of learning that can reveal new facets of the novel. The landscape of *Smith* is foreign in both time and place yet through joint experiences, readers learn something of life in eighteenth-century London at the same time that they "enjoy a good read." Garfield's cast of characters is drawn with Dickensian strokes and rich language that borders on the poetic. Some students respond to this, while others like the tension of the plot. The open-endedness of logs allows us to discuss those ideas that most intrigue readers.

Organizing the remaining responses to the literature varies with the novel and the readers, but generally class time will be divided into three sections: reading, responding through writing, and talking. Daily reading requirements can be posted and students can be asked to come prepared with their log entries to discuss their responses at the beginning of the next class. Sometimes they may read a few chapters for homework, coming to class prepared to write in their logs for approximately ten minutes. A whole-group discussion can follow this time.

Talking About the Novel

When students work in small groups, everyone has a chance to contribute to and take ownership of his or her membership in the reading community. Changing the composition of the groups assures that each member works with every other member in the class as the reading process evolves. Building such a community strengthens the bond between readers, all of whom share a common reading experience.

The charts outlined on pages 54 and 55 serve as reference points and discussion prompts throughout the process. Students, in small groups, determine questions that have been answered, may be answered, and/or will not be answered and the reasons for this. They discuss predictions — those that materialized and those that did not — and.describe the effect of each prediction on the narrative. This activity generates active construction of the text and engages students in decisions all writers make.

Reading Response Log Entries

I view the introduction to novel study as a guided process; the teacher's role in that process is that of a mentor. For this reason, I often post questions specific to the material, alerting readers to issues that demand a response. On other occasions, I draw students' attention to the guideline for responding (see page 18).

A major goal of this first shared novel is to familiarize students with ways of thinking and writing so that they will become increasingly independent readers and writers. I will use *Smith* to illustrate the sorts of ideas that can be suggested to students as they explore a novel.

1. "Meanwhile back at the ranch" episodes have students hypothesize what is happening to a character "off-stage". "Smith has been sent to prison. His document is lost. Meanwhile, what is happening to Mr. Billing?"
2. Character sketches evolve and grow with the novel's reading. As students read, they record what they learn about a character.
3. Positive and negative graphs, best used when reading a fast-paced novel, are modeled on Linda Rief's work in *Seeking Diversity*. Reading aloud to the students initial chapters of a novel allows you to work with the students to start the graph. The example that William devised illustrates the strategy.

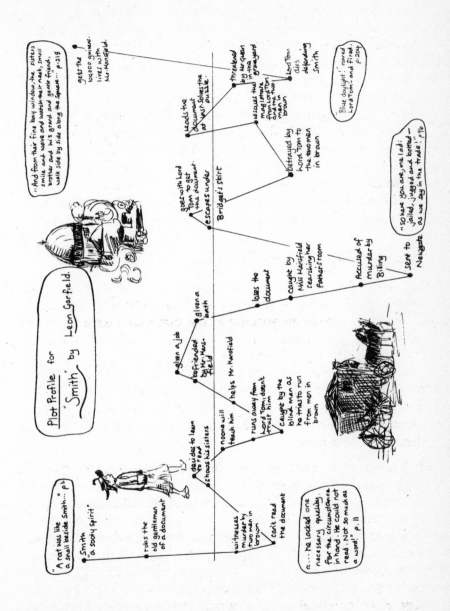

4. "Where are we?" is useful in generating words and phrases that describe a novel's settings. In the case of *Smith*, it may be the "Town," his "home," Mansfield's home, or Newgate Jail.

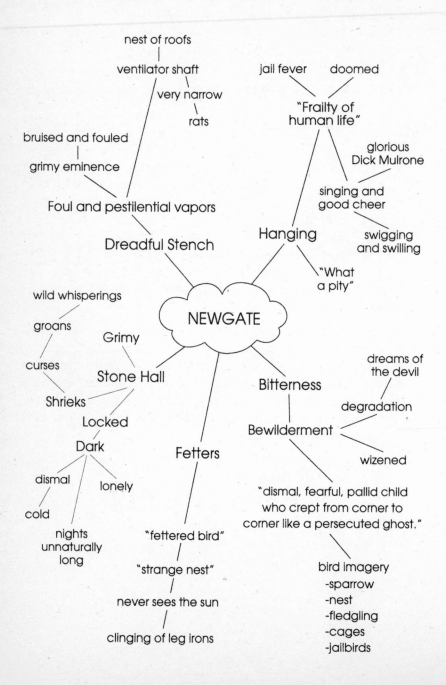

5. The strategy, "a gift of words," is useful when working with novels where language is employed in particularly effective ways. In small groups, students can select words or phrases that make an impression on them. I've used whole-class discussion time to allow each group to share a gift. Their contributions can be charted to draw further attention to the strengths of the novel's author.

Here is one example of "a gift of words".

"A rat was like a snail beside Smith, and the most his thousand or more victims ever got of him was the powerful whiff of his passing and a cold draft in their dexterously emptied pockets."

6. Sociograms help students to visualize relationships between a novel's characters. Main characters' names are printed in larger circles; those of lesser characters in smaller circles. Relationships between characters are indicated by their proximity to each other. Readers decide on the type of relationship the two characters share, and create connectors that demonstrate this relationship (e.g., blue lines for family, jagged lines for enemies). The sociogram on the next page illustrates relationships of characters in *Smith*.

7. Prediction and question charts posted earlier in the process may also serve as response prompts for students. This can include writing about a prediction that has come true or has failed to materialized, noting a characteristic of Smith's that has only recently emerged, or writing an answer to a question posed earlier. Students use their logs to respond to information as it is added to the charts.

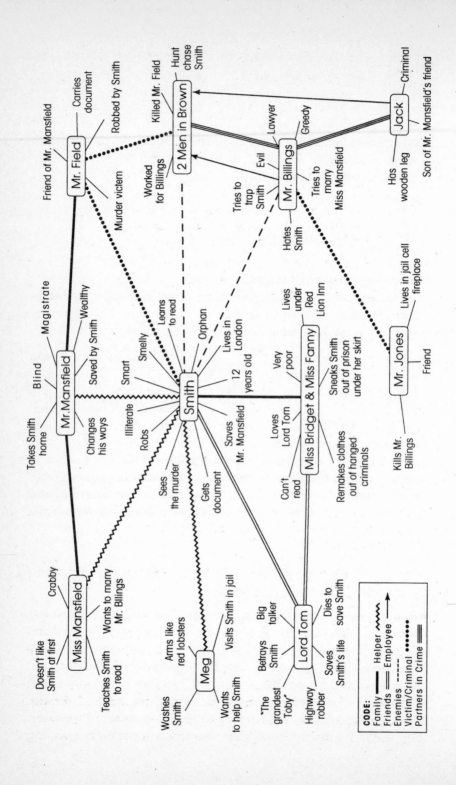

Mr. Field
 — Carries document
 — Friend of Mr. Mansfield
 — Robbed by Smith
 — Murder victem
 — Killed Mr. Field

2 Men in Brown
 — Hunt chase Smith
 — Worked for Billings
 — Tries to trap Smith
 — Evil

Mr. Billings
 — Lawyer
 — Greedy
 — Tries to marry Miss Mansfield
 — Hates Smith

Jack
 — Criminal
 — Son of Mr. Mansfield's friend
 — Has wooden leg

Mr. Jones
 — Lives in jail cell fireplace
 — Friend
 — Kills Mr. Billings

Mr. Mansfield
 — Magistrate
 — Blind
 — Wealthy
 — Saved by Smith
 — Takes Smith home
 — Changes his ways

Miss Mansfield
 — Crabby
 — Doesn't like Smith at first
 — Wants to marry Mr. Billings
 — Teaches Smith to read

Smith
 — Learns to read
 — Orphan
 — Lives in London
 — 12 years old
 — Smelly
 — Smart
 — Illiterate
 — Robs
 — Sees the murder
 — Gets document
 — Saves Mr. Mansfield
 — Loves Lord Tom

Miss Bridget & Miss Fanny
 — Very poor
 — Lives under Red Lion Inn
 — Sneaks Smith out of prison under her skirt
 — Can't read
 — Remakes clothes out of hanged criminals

Lord Tom
 — Big talker
 — "The grandest Toby"
 — Highway robber
 — Betrays Smith
 — Saves Smith's life
 — Dies to save Smith

Meg
 — Arms like red lobsters
 — Visits Smith in jail
 — Washes Smith
 — Wants to help Smith

CODE:
 — Family
 — Friends
 — Enemies
 — Helper
 — Victim/Criminal
 — Partners in Crime

Assessment and Evaluation Criteria for the Novel Unit

Before students engage in independent work, we discuss the criteria for assessment and evaluation that will be used for novel study. For this unit, these expectations typically include:

- responding actively to the novel in the log and discussions,
- demonstrating understanding of the narrative form,
- using the log during discussions,
- reading independently,
- connecting the novel to personal feelings and experiences,
- connecting the novel to other art and literature,
- showing ability to interrogate the novel,
- predicting and showing understanding of the novel,
- making judgments and comparisons,
- demonstrating growth in understanding of and appreciation for novels,
- reading more complex and challenging literature.

As suggested on page 22, logs will account for 50 marks; contributions to group and class discussions, 20; and the final product, 30. Students have the option of splitting marks for the final product in half if they choose to have their literary essay evaluated (see page 68). The essay is marked according to several factors, including the students' grasp of the topic they have explored and their ability to implement the writing process.

Knowing the criteria before they begin their independent work helps students to identify their responsibility for learning and makes them aware that assessment and evaluation occur throughout a unit.

Further Encounters with Novels: Using the Reading Response Log Independently

I wanted my Grade 9 students to read *I Am the Cheese* by Robert Cormier, a novel about "doublespeak," power, and the dramatic effect of language on people's lives. Given that the text shifts between a bike ride to Vermont, dialogues with a therapist, and flashbacks of the main character's earlier existence, I was unsure of students' reactions when asked to read the novel. I decided to have them read the entire novel during class, where they would stop reading only to record their ongoing responses in their log.

I reviewed my plan with the students, outlining that the reading period would extend for seven classes. For each response, they were reminded to date their entry, the number of pages read, and references to any specific passages that sparked a response. I reminded them, too, that they should respond on a regular basis, for example, responding at least once for every ten pages of text. To help them with their responses, I referred them to their guideline for a list of prompts (see page 18).

Each day I posted a page number on the board. Students were to read up to that page and respond to what they had read. If they could not complete their work in class, they took it home to finish for the next day. Students were aware that at the beginning of each class, I would note the page number they had read to in my record book, and that I would collect and read their logs before we discussed the novel.

My first walk around the class was revealing to say the least. In their logs, I noted many questions and a few other items.

ANNETTE: Why is his father in the hospital? How old is he and what's his name? What do the tapes mean?

KRISTA: I hate this. You can't make me do this. You call this English? I have no idea what to write so I'll just ask questions. (All my friends hate this, too!)

The second response made me grin. I pointed to the "so I'll just ask questions" part and said, "Good idea" before moving on.

So it continued until all students had finished the novel. I collected the logs and, curious about what readers had to say, began a journey that irrevocably altered my perceptions. I read and jotted responses in the margins — my surprise, questions, wonderings, reactions, and learning. I read through the evening and into the night, at times turning to my husband with a "Listen to this!" I looked forward to reading Krista's log. Her extreme, initial resistance gave way to curiosity and personal involvement. About two-thirds of the way into the response, she noted: "I am a detective. I'm searching out the clues and all the pieces are coming together!"

The students' logs showed clearly three things: their impressive depth of engagement with the novel; the levels of understandings that they reached; and the number of questions they asked (over 1000 different questions by 45 readers). They wrote an average of 8.5 pages of response (without stipulated limits).

When I handed back the logs — and this has remained constant throughout my time in response-based classrooms — students were anxious to reread them and discover how I had reacted to their work. Students value this style of personal contact and care that their ideas are taken seriously. Log comments play an important role in maintaining literary discussions.

What sort of comments do I write? There are general statements and questions that can be made or asked of any book, and there are specific statements and questions that are determined by the particular text under discussion. Here are examples of general responses to students' reflections that I use:

- I never thought of this before.
- Can you answer this question now?
- Why do you feel this happened?
- Ask this question in your group discussion.
- This puzzles me too. Ask others.
- I wonder if I would do this?
- What if the author had chosen your prediction? What would have happened to the story?
- Why do you think this is significant?
- Tell me more about this.
- What do you think will be the outcome of this?
- I wonder what you would do in this situation.

Some comments affirm for students that they are on the right track; others push them to explore their thinking. My responses may open windows to new understanding, or make suggestions about which points would be fruitful for further discussion.

The next step is to form small discussion groups and talk. *I Am the Cheese* provoked animated discussion. I could not keep the students from waving their books, asking questions, and demanding answers with support from the text. One group of boys, stuffing the paperback in their pockets, continued their discussions outside. What a Pandora's box I had opened! These discussions had a liveliness and scope that I had never witnessed in the classroom. Could the time taken to read, think, and respond to the literature have so radically altered the talk that followed? My curiosity led me to videotape future class discussions.

George Orwell's *Animal Farm* proved the perfect book for this next step. The following is a partial transcript of the first discussion to be held after students had read the book, responded in their logs, and read my response to their work. No background information had been distributed to the students, although they had the chance to read the logs of two or three classmates.

ADAM: Yeah. I noticed that they were breaking the commandments, too.

MEGAN: It was so slowly and gradually... that's the pits.

NIEVE: They were breaking them. They were writing up new ones.

ADAM: New ones.

MEGAN: But that's just it. It sounds really stupid. But have you noticed like in life? How people do that? They're like, they're hypocritical?

LEE: They set things and then...

MEGAN: They say, "I don't want you to, You can't do this" and then they do it themselves and they make it look like it's okay.

ADAM: Yeah.

MEGAN: This is like, I put in here, it's about politics because it's like leaders. The pigs are the leaders but they're leading the blind and dumb because they don't think for themselves. They just go, you know.

NIEVE: That's what communism's all about. They had one leader like when they had elected him as president. There's only one candidate.

LEE: What's the use of having an election, really?

MEGAN: Even though they found out that they didn't like it.

NIEVE: To make people think they had a choice. Yeah, they didn't think they'd have a choice because they'd die.

MEGAN: That's how it was with Hitler. If they weren't soldiers for his army then they'd kill them. I think that's how they felt. But in the end, I think that they should have just left or killed him. I don't think...

LEE: They'd have had a riot then. Killed off Napoleon. It would have been a better story.

ADAM: I think it got confusing at the end.

NIEVE: Yeah.

MEGAN: I think it sort of answered itself from the beginning. It circled over and over.

LEE: I don't get this. The humans understand animals. That's stupid. That's really dumb.

ADAM: And when they sang that "Beasts of England" song then all the humans could understand them.

MEGAN: How could they hear them? They couldn't hear them before.

LEE: Yeah, really.

MEGAN: And some of the adults were stupid. They couldn't, they can't write or anything.

LEE: Yeah. They wouldn't do that. Like when they had that riot thing. They wouldn't go into a garden, I wouldn't go into a garden and take a gun. They're going to be rushing in and turn me into pulp or something.

MEGAN: Yeah, I know.

LEE: That's really dumb.

What excites me about these discussions? Three aspects are important: the talk process, talk strategies, and the content of the discussion. Students stay on task and are committed to the talk. Their discussion is interactive and animated, and resembles real-life conversations about texts. It is dynamic, moving through different topics as one remark leads to another. Students maintain momentum by choosing their own topics for discussion. Like real talk, there is an element of tentativeness as students formulate ideas at the same time that they give voice to them.

As students talk, they undergo a process of mutual discovery and affirmation ("New ones," "Yeah, really," and "The humans understand animals"). They connect their own experiences to the novel ("But have you noticed like in life?") and connect this to what they already know ("That's how it was with Hitler"). They interpret ("It's about politics") and generalize ("That's what communism's all about," "What's the use of having an election, really?"). They begin to discuss the structure of the novel ("I think it sort of answered itself from the beginning. It circled over and over") and they challenge the author's consistency in the novel ("How could they hear them? They couldn't hear them before").

The content of the discussion ranges from "breaking the commandments" to personal experience, structure, and consistency, and touches on the novel's major themes of communism, elections, and leadership. As well, students begin to analyze the characters ("They're leading the blind and dumb because they don't think for themselves").

This kind of talk is valuable because it informs us, as teachers, about the nature and level of the students' involvement with the novel and points to recurrent questions and problems that arise. We can then make informed decisions about further instruction.

Students are also aware of the benefits of "talking through" the novel with peers. When asked to reflect on the process of discussing a novel in groups, students made these comments.

LEE: When you work in the groups, you can tell what people are thinking. I may not agree with it but it's still a valid opinion. In some of it, I mean, it's something that I missed and look, you see how they saw it and it's something else you can put down.

ADAM: When you've got other people asking you questions, you kind of have to challenge yourself and think things through.

NIEVE: Others took things out of the book that I didn't notice.

MEGAN: The questions that I had were answered right away. The discussion put in some of the missing pieces I just couldn't get by myself.

These experiences have convinced me that it is not only worthwhile but essential to take class time to read and write. Given this belief, I was more than dismayed when one teacher said, "I felt guilty actually just reading and writing in school." Imagine! Guilt about reading and writing in school! What reading and writing in class time offers us is a glimpse into the response processes and strategies our students use to read a novel. What we find often stimulates and informs us, and we come to know real readers. More importantly, the act of writing before talking means that no one comes to the group unprepared or unrehearsed.

The Literary Essay

The literary essay was certainly a staple in my class, but my own shift in teaching literature led me to rethink the issue of essays and for that matter, all activities that typically followed the reading of a novel. I began to read about essays, which means to try, an attempt. I was ready to move beyond "Write a 500-word essay: Compare Snowball and Napoleon in *Animal Farm*," but I wasn't ready to abandon the form entirely.

I began by comparing essays that students had written after reading a book and doing questions and quizzes with those done by students who had responded in logs. By far the most interesting, distinct, and varied writing came from a Grade 10 class who had read *The Chrysalids* while using a log. The students' teacher, Liz, asked them to read through their logs and note questions, problems, or issues that interested them or that remained unresolved. From this exercise, each student chose a topic she or he wanted to explore. The next class was devoted to writing an in-class essay on the topic of their choice; students were able to use their log if they wished. All 27 students came prepared to write an essay, and wrote without stopping for 50 minutes. A tally of the essays revealed 22 topics, among them "Who is Uncle Axel?" "The Powers of the Children," and "Religion in The Chrysalids." The content and quality of the writing surprised us, and Liz commented on the natural, coherent language found in the essays. Readers seemed personally involved in their writing. Here is Alison's assessment of the character Joseph.

Joseph Strom is a character in the book *The Chrysalids* by John Wyndham. He is the father of David. Joseph is close-minded and very grumpy. He has things his way or no way at all. Joseph is temperamental, judgmental, and is inflexible with his judgements. In the story, David had gotten a splinter in his hand. He pulled it out and it bled a lot. David tried to tie a rag around it but it was too hard. He said "that if he had another hand he could have managed it by himself." Joseph took it the wrong way and thought he was wishing for another hand, when in fact he just simply made a statement. His father yelled at him and cursed him saying how could he wish for such a devilish thing? He said that David had blasphemed and that he should go to his room. Joseph didn't let David explain that he was just stating a fact. Joseph just blew up and told him to get on his knees and pray. Joseph is a narrow minded creep. He doesn't let anybody say anything. He assumes the worst or what he thinks is the worst. I would not like to be in the predicament that David is in.

This model demonstrates the need for the essay to return to its roots as an "attempt" to think through an issue by writing. First-draft writing, done in limited time, can reveal much about a student's level of understanding.

There are occasions where a more deliberate process is appropriate. To have readers think deeply about their response to a novel through a formal writing assignment needs time, supervision, and intentional teaching. The greatest difference in writing occurs when we lead students through the process.

I teach using mini-lessons — five-minute demonstrations of a pertinent strategy or process — at the beginning of each class. Examples of lesson topics include using the log to assemble information, choosing an essay topic, using quotes, finding resources, proofreading, and publishing. Students keep all draft writing and notes about mini-lessons in the log. They then have a practical, accessible record of their essays as they evolve.

Students survey their logs for potential essay topics. They generate these as well as questions, themes, and issues that they want to explore and underline all related responses in their logs. On occasion, they can chart their findings for the whole class to consider. One student captured the essence of the process when he said, ''... it puts your ideas into perspective as you do it [the log]. It's much easier to grasp an idea [for an essay] instead of trying to think over the whole book in your mind, trying to pick out certain key elements. This way you have it already right there!''

Encourage students to web or list as many words related to the topic as they can in three to five minutes. A 10-minute free-write where students record non-stop for up to 10 minutes their feelings, issues, and questions on a topic is another great way to assemble ideas and generate writing. The students' goal in these situations is to write as much as possible (asking them to keep the pen on paper at all times greatly aids this activity) without worrying about order, spelling, or grammar.

Once students have completed this process, they are ready to tackle the first draft of an essay. The writing then follows the steps of the writing process with revisions, editing, proofreading, preparing the final draft, and finally, sharing their essay with others. This last phase is an important part of the process since the completed essays need to have a function beyond being read and graded by a teacher. I have compiled class books of essays that have been read by subsequent classes. Sometimes, we form small groups where each member reads the same essay so that it may be used as the basis for a final discussion of the novel.

Extending the Novel Experience: Forming Book Clubs

Students should now be ready to work in small groups with a variety of novels. To help them form book clubs, I lead students through a process that involves ranking the novels I have selected for this portion of the unit by their titles and then by their synopses. In both instances, students rank the novels on a scale from 1 (low) to 10 (high) and write a one- or two-sentence response.

After ranking the titles, students form small groups where they explain their choices. They remain in the groups to listen to the synopses, repeating the ranking and discussion processes. Often, the ranking will alter radically after the synopses have been read. Students can record reasons for their change of mind and what decided them on one novel above others before they confirm to the group their choice.

I then print the titles of the novels on separate sheets of paper or on chart paper. Students, by signing up for the novel they want to read, form book clubs. Clubs should contain no more than five members; if more than five students are interested in reading the same novel, I ask them to form two clubs of relative size.

While I set a general reading deadline for finishing the novels, each book club sets its own mini-agenda — how many pages will be read per day, how responses will be shared, and what percentage of class time will be set aside for discussion. Ask each club for a copy of its agenda so that you can monitor progress at the beginning of each class. Logs can be collected at the end of the reading period.

When members of each club have completed their reading, they need to decide on how they will share their novel with other clubs. Some may act out a scene, others will present a radio play, still others will introduce their novel's characters and problems to the rest of the class. Class time devoted to planning the presentations and supportive mini-lessons can help students with this component of the unit. The point of this time is to have readers focus on central issues in the novel and invite others to read it.

A final method for sharing information about novels involves having students form jigsaw groups where each member tells others about the novel his or her group read. Students then sign up to read their next novel based on recommendations they heard in their jigsaw group.

Independent Novel Study: The Reading Workshop

After several stabs at independent reading, I have found that a class library of paperbacks housed on spinners works best for this phase of novel study. The paperbacks can belong to the class, or can be on loan from the school library for a one-month period.

The whole issue of controlling selections for student reading is, for me at least, a red herring. When readers progress through the stages I have outlined in this chapter, reading selection is better left to them. To be sure, I exert some influence by selecting books to be placed in the spinner but choice by the reader is an important step in the continuing reading of adolescents. Their independent choices provide a context for conferencing or suggesting other related books. To know what a reader selects independently represents another way we can learn about him or her.

Individual conferences can take place while students are engaged in silent reading and writing. Students who have completed a novel can sign up for a teacher conference. If they have questions they want to discuss during the conference, they can note them at the end of their log entries. At the time of the conference or shortly after, I record the discussion in my record book. The following examples of prompts help me to carry on a discussion about reading with my students. Questions pertinent to a specific book are developed as we encounter each text.

- Why did you choose this book? Was it a good choice? What sort of book did you think it was going to be?
- Tell me about your reading experience with this book. What did you especially like or dislike?
- What is your immediate response toward the book?
- Do you want to continue reading it? Why/why not? Were there parts that bored you? If you have stopped reading, where did you stop and what stopped you?
- Have you read other books like this? How are they the same? How does this book compare to other novels you have read?
- Would you recommend this novel to others? What would you tell them about the book? What would you not tell them?
- How do the characters and/or events connect with your own experience?
- Will you discuss this book with another student? Why? Why not?
- Would you read another book by this author or in this genre?

Class Share

As the independent reading progresses, a class bulletin board can be filled with book titles, diagrams, quotes, references, book reviews, recommendations, and information about authors and genres. These "tidbits" can be used to aid discussions and class sharings of novels members of the class have read.

At the end of each class, students can contribute something about the book they are reading to the whole group. At other times, they can organize into small groups where each student talks about his or her novel. Both of these types of discussion focus on sharing stories and looking for similarities and differences between novels and authors. Questions of style may be posted for discussion to be answered by each student, particularly if she or he is reading a genre such as science fiction.

Bringing It All Together: Evaluation Activities

These concluding activities, to be done on an individual basis save one, will account for either 15 percent (the student has submitted an essay for evaluation) or 30 percent of the final mark for the unit. The unit can end with each student presenting his or her work to the rest of the class.

1. Draw a map that represents a journey undertaken by a character. Significant events from the plot, page references, and quotes can also be included.
2. Create a family tree that includes friendships, influences, and interests, as well as blood ties.
3. Draw a film storyboard for one scene. Each frame of the storyboard should indicate a change in camera slot.
4. Create a package for a novel that includes a new book jacket, advertising "blurb," and copies of reviews and posters.
5. Write a front-page newspaper report on one incident from the novel.
6. Research and write a television script about a major issue in the novel.
7. Write, in role, a character's reactions to an event.
8. Make a soundtrack that represents a scene in the novel or establishes setting.

CHAPTER FOUR

Poetry — The Best Words in the Best Order

Our English Department head laughed uproariously when I suggested "doing" poetry with the non-academic students — Ed among them. "Now call me in when that happens! I want to be there for that!" he mocked. I was admittedly taken aback but not deterred. Instead, it made me more determined than ever to explore poetry with all students.

I hadn't always felt that way. I remember the sense of awe when high school teachers and later university professors would reveal the hidden depths, symbols, and abstract meanings of a poem we were studying. I felt no connection to the work and certainly no predisposition or ability to analyze it. I took meticulous notes and felt relegated to the role of intellectual midget.

Out of class I read and enjoyed poetry, rereading some poems, memorizing portions of others, and incorporating poetic words and phrases in my speech. And I wrote poetry in high school — long, romantic, rhymed versions of the human condition — generally my own and generally having to do with pain or love. Later, I used poetry to explore in more depth personal feelings and experiences. I loved poetry, but not the way it had been taught.

This changed as a result of a professor in an English Education class. Here, the professor demonstrated poetry — we heard it read aloud, and we dramatized it, discussed it, made guesses about it, and wrote about it. This was the connection between my poetry experiences as a student and how I wanted my students to experience it. My formal, rather lackluster experience as a student of poetry strengthened my resolve to bring poetry alive for my students. I wanted them to know that they had a right to read poetry and respond personally. Paul Valery said, "I write half the poem. The reader writes the other half." The first part was obvious; the second challenged me to create contexts for each reader to "write the second half."

Introducing Poetry: Strategies that Work Using the Reading Response Log

The following strategies have proved effective over the years. They introduce students to poetry in a non-threatening, positive light that shows them poetry can be enjoyable, a sentiment all too many of us never experienced in our school years.

Puzzle Poems

A timely piece of advice came from a colleague: "Begin your poetry with something painless," she said. I decided to begin with puzzle poems (poems that make no mention of the topic in the body of the poem). I walked into the class, distributed a copy of Sylvia Plath's "Mushrooms" with the title removed, and asked students to organize into small response groups. Each group was asked to elect a member to read the poem aloud. Once they had a chance to listen to the poem, they began to generate a list of possible titles. For each title, students reread the poem to check for "fit."

As the list grew longer, students read and reread the poem repeatedly. Possibilities included: snow, frost, worms, trees, atom bombs, youth, weeds, mold, plants, termites, sunflowers, and dandelions.

To illustrate the process, I have included a transcript of one group's work with the poem. Students sought to uncover the title by fitting the pieces together until it made sense for them. In such cases, the talk is a process of meaning making, and students are the ones making the meanings.

JEN: Shelves and tables aren't really shelves and tables, they're things you can place things on.

JOHN: It's snow — look — nudgers and shovers welting the cracks — widening the crannies — snow breaks rocks apart.

VERNA: What's your guess Joel?

JOEL: I think snow — it fits snow perfectly.

JEN: No. Snow is too literal.

JOHN: There's the same qualities as snow — overnight — take hold of the loam—diet on water...

JEN: Yeah and things are overlooked until they're missing — you know like toilet paper — you don't notice it 'til its gone — like snow.

WILL: Could be death itself — white light — a near-death experience.

VERNA: So how far are we?

JOHN: Termites — snow.

VERNA: Youth — I'm sticking to that.

JOHN: It could be ice — crumbs of shadow.

WILL: Or plants and trees — they grow toward the light.

JOHN: Gotta have nudgers and shovers — does everything fit?

JEN: Meek — shelves and tables are.

WILL: But from a tree's point of view slow it all down — all the plants are still there.

JOHN: Overnight? Whitely?

JOEL: It's a riddle — remember the Sphinx?

When the time was up, groups reported their final guesses, and reasons for these guesses, to the rest of the class. Some groups were in consensus; others were not. Some groups asked questions and challenged the choices: "What about 'we are edible?'" to a guess of trees, or worms. After final guesses were posted on the board, students were anxious to know what the author called the poem. Using the phrase, "The author chose to call it 'Mushrooms'" relieved them of some of the pressure of having to be right.

One of the best log responses came directly after this experience. Readers were asked to put their poems aside and record as many words or phrases that they could remember from the poem. Many recalled those that had stumped them: "we are shelves, we are tables," "our foot's in the door," or "we are edible." The opening, for most, was easy to remember: "Overnight, whitely, quietly" as was "diet on water," "crannies," "so many of us," and "bland-mannered." When the time was up, students compared their memories with others in the group and added to their original list. They put the words and phrases in order by numbering them or cutting them out. Finally, students were able to compare their ordered words and phrases to the original poem.

To bring closure, students were asked to do a 10- to 15-minute written "impression" of the poem in their logs: How effective was the poem in describing mushrooms? What did they think about the poem's language? What was the poem's most striking aspect? What image did the poem present to them? Here's an example written by Kevin, a Grade 9 student.

"The mushrooms are thinking to themselves that they are
perfect and they are coming out of the ground to take over
the earth. They come out of the soil and smell the air. Soft
fists moving needles; mushrooms are soft and can be
squashed easily but they push themselves through the ground
and push the grass out of the way. They come out through
silent holes that widen as they push. 'We shall by morning
inherit the earth'—'our foot's in the door'—the mushrooms
think they're going to take over the earth; they have been put
there; 'little or nothing so many of us'—whether you care or
not the mushrooms are there and there's a lot of them.
Something is out there slowly invading us. Mushroom;
mighty powerful pushes through the ground; threatens the
ground; multiplying; war on soil. Atom bomb; mushroom
cloud; weapon threatens us; multiplying; war on us. Just a
thought. And somehow, the poem reminds me of *Lord of the
Rings.*"

This kind of writing asks readers to dig deeply into their experience with the poem and to express their response and growing
understanding and appreciation. These qualities are hard to come
by when we teachers "do" the analysis for them!

After visiting a school and demonstrating this strategy to a
Grade 10 class, I overheard students discussing the poem in the
hallway. One student met a student from another Grade 10 class
and said, "If you have a visitor in your class today and she gives
you a poem, the title is 'Mushrooms!'" I smiled and pulled out
another for the next class! Because readers enjoy the "puzzle"
aspect of the poems, they often ask for more. I have used "The
Base Stealer" by Robert Francis and "Filling Station" by A.M.
Klein in a similar fashion.

Playing with Words

Because poems are "the best words in the best order," I usually
move from puzzle poems to a set of poems where selected words
have been padded with synonyms. A good example of this type
of poem is Tennyson's "The Eagle." With the opening, "He clasps
the crag with crooked hands" the effect is clear. When "grabs"
and "clenches" are added to "clasps"; when "bent" and
"twisted" are added to "crooked"; and when "talons" and
"claws" are added to "hands," then students must decide what
is the "best word" for the poem. The first line of "The Eagle"
might look like this:

	grabs				crooked	claws
He	clenches	the	crag	with	bent	hands
	clasps				twisted	talons

Students gather in small groups to deliberate their choices. They read and re-read the poem to get an image in their minds, perhaps sketching what they "see" as they think about the picture the poem presents. They debate, argue, agree, and finally, write in their logs the words they have selected as the most powerful or fitting for the poem. I ask them to spend two minutes writing a reflection on what they think of the words.

JOHN: I see the eagle, high above the sea, wind ruffling his feathers. The yellow eyes watching every detail. Then from the rocks he dives, down to the world below.

WILLIAM: Twisted (my choice) gives a greater impression of age. "Crooked" is a bit sinister, not like the vision of the eagle as a rational symbol of goodness, light, and nobility. "Wrinkled" gives a feeling of distance and separation.

VERNA: I see a picture of an eagle looking straight at a fish and then pouncing on it. I don't like wrinkled sea beneath him crawls — it fits the rhyme scheme but I associate wrinkles with old and crawling with young. That brings a conflict. What the heck does "Ringed with the azure world, he stands" mean?

I ask each group to reach a consensus on the poem members most like. Each small group then reports their choice by reading it aloud. Some groups will designate a leader; some will read the poem chorally; some will share or distribute lines to be read aloud. Groups have the chance to defend their decisions and challenge those made by others. Since "The Eagle," for example, uses an "aaa/bbb" rhyme scheme, readers may argue that the word "talons" doesn't fit the scheme. Typically, readers become attached to their version of the poem and argue strongly in defense of their selections — a process poets use in their poems. By the time students have read Tennyson's words, they have produced a strong, powerful understanding of the image he presents.

Many poems can be treated in this way. I have used "Ozymandius" by Shelley, "Snake" by D.H. Lawrence, and "Tarantella" by Hilaire Belloc. In all cases, students derive the greatest benefit from the process when they work in small groups to decide on the best choice of words. Together, they come to appreciate that word choice in poetry is intentional and that poetry is a craft.

Filming a Poem

A dramatic follow-up to playing with words, as suggested by Mike Hayhoe, is for students to create a plan for making a short film of the poem. They do this by mapping how each line from the poem can be presented visually and/or with sound. They begin by pasting the following filming codes on the left-hand side of a page in their log.

```
                      FILMING CODES

WA        wide angle (e.g., country scene)
FF        full frame (e.g., whole person, object)
HF        half frame (e.g., half body/object)
CU        close-up (e.g., face, hand, ring)
ZI/ZO     zoom in/out (e.g., towards CU or away from CU
          to FF)
TU/TD     tilt up/down (e.g., from ground level upward
          or from height down)
P         Pan — move camera in circular sweep
T         Track — move parallel to moving object
```

Students then make a worksheet to use when planning the film. The worksheet can appear on the right-hand side of the page, facing the codes and include these heads: pictures, film code, quotation from poem, comment, and music/sound effect.

There are several ways groups of students can work to complete this activity. One tack is to have them create the "film" on paper; another is to have them create a slide or film presentation. Using computers provides students with additional flexibility and room to create. Whatever method or equipment they use, group presentations are invariably dynamic and each will bear a unique stamp.

As a culminating activity, students describe in their logs what happened to their vision, understanding, and appreciation of a poem through this experience.

Explorations Through Performance:
Read Aloud and More

Poetry is meant to be read aloud. A poem's flow of language, its narrative, its sounds, and its rhythms come alive in a good reading. After my students have had some initial experiences with poetry, I begin to immerse them in the read-aloud experience. Using taped and filmed poetry readings, as well as our own voices, we begin to appreciate the special way in which language is used in poetry. I read aloud; and students read aloud in numerous ways, including choral readings and role-playing presentations.

When selecting poetry to read aloud or perform, it is wise to take into account the nature of the class and provide for a range of styles and types by including humorous, narrative, rhymed, free-verse, traditional, and modern poems, and poems for solo, paired, and choral readings.

Effective oral presentation requires thought and preparation. Reading poetry aloud requires several elements, including practice in timing the reading; marking punctuation to avoid the "sing-song" style so often heard in rhymed poetry; and making marginal notes to slow, speed up, stress words or phrases, change tone or volume, and attend to the feelings evoked by the words.

Choral speaking performances of poems may be a small-group assignment that adds a new dimension to understanding a work. In order to read aloud effectively, students must pay attention to the possible meanings in a poem. Given that there will be divergence of opinion on the part of members, lively discussion is usually a part of this activity and should be looked upon as a vital component of preparing for a performance.

My students love drama and performing, and will take turns role playing a poem's characters or narrator. Other students then interview the role-playing students, asking about their experiences and the events, feelings, and motives expressed in the poem. This helps students to engage with ideas that are inferential, rather than explicit. An alternative to this approach is to ask the character(s) to describe themselves, the ideas and feelings expressed in the poem, and/or what happened before and after the poem. Having students sit in a semi-circle so that all can see one another works particularly well for this sort of activity.

Responding to Poetry Read Aloud

The log has an important role to play in helping students to develop ideas about the poems we encounter in class. Before we hear a poem read aloud or watch it performed, students can record in their log its title and the poet's name. Asking them what they think the poem will be about or what image is suggested by its title can help them to generate initial impressions. Taking a few minutes to jot down these impressions also appears to help students attend more closely to the poem when it is read.

Depending on how the poem is presented, students listen or watch the poem performed. At its end, they respond to the poem in any way they wish, perhaps writing a list of words that struck them, making a sketch, or engaging in a freewrite. Students can also rank the poem on a scale of 1 (low) to 5 (high), explain their ranking, and provide a comment about the poem and the presentation. What struck them about this poem? Were they able to get involved in the presentation? What could be improved? What other ways might there be for presenting this poem? Students share their reflections and responses in small groups before gathering to form a large group. Finally, the class experiences the poem as a whole group.

While the number of poems presented at this stage will vary, the goal should be to introduce enough poems to students that they develop an appetite for them, experience a variety of styles, and feel secure in starting to explore their personal responses without the weight of detailed analysis. At all costs, we want to avoid making poetry so complicated and intimidating that students will shun it.

Assessment and Evaluation Criteria for the Poetry Unit

For this unit, marks for taking part in discussions (20 percent) and completing a final activity (30 percent) are based on student self-evaluation and teacher evaluation. As a guide to rating performance in discussions, students can complete the survey on page 31. Evaluation of the logs (50 percent) will be based on your evaluation only. The following list provides a comprehensive overview of the goals of poetry teaching and is useful for assessing and evaluating the learning:

- appreciates poetry as a literary form,
- enjoys reading poetry,
- reads poetry for personal reading,
- becomes involved and engaged in poetry,
- understands the forms and functions of poetry,
- gains wide experience in poetry reading,
- understands the range of forms and structure in poetry,
- discusses poetry knowledgeably with others,
- withholds final/decisive interpretations,
- explores possible meanings,
- discusses poetry to uncover meanings,
- articulates understanding and response in writing,
- understands and uses the terminology of poetry.

Moving Toward Individual Choices Using the Reading Response Log

Having experienced as a class several poems and worked through strategies such as puzzle poems, students are now ready to take part in more individualized activities. A good way for them to begin this segment of the unit is to start a personal collection of poems they enjoy — song lyrics, poems that they have read, enjoyed, or written, poems they enjoyed as children, and lines they have memorized. As students copy, paste, and write poems in their logs, and explain the inclusion of each poem, the logs become repositories of their encounters with poetry. Shane wrote, "I picked this poem because my grandmother read this to me every time she came to visit when I was small because, she said, 'Shane, this reminds me of you. The same kind of crazy imagination.' If I want to remember her, I read 'And to Think That I Saw It on Mulberry Street.'"

Janelle loved cats and read and reread T.S. Eliot's "Old Possum's Book of Practical Cats." She went to the Broadway production of "Cats" and wrote, "I could sing along with many of the songs because they were already so familiar to me. My favorite one is "The Rum Tum Tigger" because it reminds me of my cat — "For he will do/As he do do/And there's no doing anything about it!" Ken brought in lyrics by Jimi Hendrix; Stacy a set of poems she had written about moving to Canada from Hong Kong. Tracey brought in Roald Dahl's "Revolting Rhymes" and wrote that she thought the poems were "hilarious" because "they use something so familiar to us (fairy tales) and give a very funny twist to them." I read "Little Red Riding Hood and the Wolf" using an English accent to try out for the Thespians in school — and made it! My favorite part of the poem is:

> Then Little Red Riding Hood said, 'But Grandma,
> what a lovely great big furry coat you have on.'
> 'That's wrong!' cried Wolf. 'Have you forgot
> 'To tell me what BIG TEETH I've got?'
> 'Ah well, no matter what you say,
> 'I'm going to eat you anyway.'
> The small girl smiles. One eyelid flickers.
> She whips a pistol from her knickers.
> She aims it at the creature's head
> And bang bang bang, she shoots him dead.

When students have collected a number of their favorite poems, you can invite them to sit in a circle and read one to the rest of the group. Students talk about why they chose their poem, and as they read aloud other students will give inevitable signs of recognition, chuckles, and nods: "I remember that poem," "That was my favorite song in Grade 8," or "I had to memorize that poem. I never liked daffodils again after that."

Anthology Browse: The Top Twenty

Students, as part of a four-person group, read through anthologies and note in their logs titles they like, noting poets' names and relevant page numbers. They continue until, as a group, they have a total of 20 poems. Each member then chooses their five favorites and writes a brief reason why they selected these poems. Members share their choices and rationale before deciding on the group's "top five" poems. This is often the most difficult part of the activity since consensus is rarely easily achieved. If interest remains high, the class can create a "Top 20" poems chart.

Using the Reading Response Log to Deepen Appreciation

Students have now reached the point where they are ready to tackle a challenging poem. To help them make sense of poems where meanings are hidden beneath the surface, I give students the following guide.

A TEN-POINT GUIDE TO READING POETRY

1. Keep an open mind. Forget about what the poem may mean or what it may be about.
2. Look at the title. What does it suggest to you? Jot down in your log your ideas and suggestions from your group.
3. Read the poem aloud several times to absorb its overall idea and feeling.
4. Try to hear the words. Poems make sounds as well as patterns on the page.
5. Record anything that strikes your eye, your ear, or your interest. Examples might be: unusual words, strange word order, rhymes, rhythms, layout, puzzling passages, unusual punctuation, heavy use of adverbs or adjectives — or their absence, verb tense, and verb type — action or emotion.
5. Look for clusters in the language. Jot down any words or phrases that seem to belong together or to echo one another. As an example, there might be words about sorrow throughout a poem "grief/tears/heavy eyes/tight-wrung handkerchief" or similes and metaphors might cluster around an idea — the ferocity of an animal, the harshness of winter, and so on.
6. Read the entire poem again.
7. Record things the poem reminds you of — memories, associations, previous reading experiences.
8. Review and discuss your notes with your group members. Now is the time to start thinking about what the poem is trying to say.
9. Tackle the following questions about the poem:
   - What voice is used in the poem? Do you think it is that of the poet or someone the poet has invented to speak through?
   - Is the intended audience a specific person or people unknown to the poet?
   - What is the poet's attitude toward his or her audience?
   - Does the poet organize the poem in a specific way? If yes, why do you think she or he has done this?
   - What part have your notes played in helping you understand the poem?
10. Read the poem a final time to "put it all together."

Patrick Dias and Michael Hayhoe (1988) recommend that we give challenging poems to small groups of students and help them on their way by reading the first part of the poem aloud. Students can pick up where we leave off, reading the poem aloud as a group, having one person read the poem aloud, or reading the poem silently. Discussion will soon follow as students ask themselves what strikes them about the poem, what words they like, what questions they have, and what the poet is trying to say. When discussion halts, one student can read the poem aloud to the rest of the group. After a specified period of time, each group (on a rotating basis and starting with Group 1, Day 1, and so on) can report on their poem to the whole group.

Students need to bring their personal experience to bear on what they read in order to find meaning in a text. To help them cross this bridge, I have them describe the poem and then read it aloud to themselves. When they have written their reflections of the experience in their logs, I ask the students if the reading evoked any personal emotions. This leads to a sharing of stories, often brief, sometimes moving, but always leading us to the question, "What is the poet saying to us?" In small groups, students talk their way through the poem; individually, each student writes what she or he observes from the poem and from other students. A group may reread the entire poem or parts of it. An important question — "How do you know that?" — brings each interpretation back to a reading of the words on the page.

Log entries made during these discussions are collected for presentation to the whole class. While one group reports on its poem, members of the other groups can add to their notes, challenge the presenting group's observations or interpretations, and ask its members questions about the presentation. The work of each group builds on the presentations of earlier groups.

Another effective strategy is what I call the "three-questions approach." All students are given a copy of the same poem and are asked to find a partner. Together, each pair of students jots down three questions they have about the poem. One set of students joins another, making groups of four. This new group selects three questions from the members' six original questions. This activity fosters considerable small-group discussion as members determine the questions they deem most important. All questions are then pooled, and the whole class works to establish common threads and solutions to the problems.

"Color underlining" is another strategy that provides for variety in poetry study. As in the three questions approach, each student is given a copy of the same poem. They form small groups and are given a colored pen to underline particular aspects of a poem; for example, one group underlines all references to setting in green, a second group underlines all references to people in red, a third group underlines all references to mood in blue, and a fourth group underlines key words and phrases in purple. Groups gather to compare underlinings, often discovering that the same words and phrases are underlined for different aspects of the poem. This strategy can also be used for spotting poetic techniques (e.g., alliteration, metaphor, simile, rhyme). An overhead projector allows groups to present their ideas to the whole class. Great discussions on elements of poems can follow!

Sometimes I want students to work individually, and have found Thomas Newkirk's suggestion for a more formal paper on poetry useful. Calling the approach "questioning the text," I provide each student with a poem we have not encountered in class and ask them to create a "reading narrative" by marking words or expressions that strike or confuse them and by writing any observations or questions in the margins. In their logs, students note shifts in their understanding as they complete additional readings of the poem. For each reading, they mark the poem with a different writing tool to provide a clear set of "tracks." After several readings, they write a brief paper (300—400 words) describing their journey through the poem.

As their comfort level and experience grows, students can be introduced to a number of poems linked by theme. Small groups of two or three students can explore and present their responses to a poem they have worked with.

"Poetry Is..."

The more experience students have, the more they can contribute to a "Poetry Is..." chart. What is poetry? How is it the same as other forms of literature? How is it different? How do you recognize poetry? Working in small groups to brainstorm characteristics of poetry and using their logs as an information base prepares students for contributing to this whole-class project. When groups take turns contributing to the chart, it is often surprising to discover how much students have learned about poetry. This list was prepared by a Grade 10 class:

POETRY IS . . .

Looking through a broken window.
Using words like azure when blue would do.
The word form of life.
Writing about emotions the way that novels write about life.
It's the Morse code of life.
A bunch of words on paper to confuse people because adults hate teenagers.
Completely subjective — you can't mark poetry.
In the eyes of the beholder.
It comes from somewhere inside, not from a rule book.

Poetry is simile
metaphor
personification
irony
humor
sound

Creating Poetry

When I worked at a school for young offenders, one student who had not written a word in the first six weeks of our program told me he had written lyrics to many songs — his own unique form of rap. Another student told me that she'd filled a whole journal with her poetry. Writing poetry can be stimulating, even for the most reluctant readers. For others, the idea of a pattern or form gives them the confidence to try their hand at writing.

A book that offers multiple strategies for helping students write their own poetry is *Poetry in the Making* by Ted Hughes. On the next pages are three poetry writing strategies I have used successfully with students.

My own love of poetry continues to grow as I meet new poems and revisit old friends through the eyes of each new generation of students. I have learned that teaching poetry is about holding back my own ideas and allowing students to tell me theirs. It's about listening to their voices as they discuss poetry among themselves, and it's about giving them opportunities to visit and revisit poems by reading them aloud. Often there is nothing more to the teaching of poetry than learning to enjoy it. As my Grade 10 students told me, "Poetry is in the eye of the beholder."

Imitative Poems

One successful strategy for involving students in poetry writing is through imitative poetry. An often-used example would be an "apology" poem using William Carlos William's "This is just to say" (e.g., "This is just to say/ I have borrowed the dress you were saving for the prom..." or "This is just to say/ I have taken the car that you left in the garage...").

In their logs, students can write a draft of their poem and read it to a partner to see how it sounds. Based on their partner's reactions, they may decide to incorporate their suggestions in a revision or follow their own judgment in deciding what needs to be altered. Revised poems can be collected and placed in a class booklet or literary magazine to be shared during a public poetry reading and/or silent reading time.

Image Poems

Some of the best poems my students have written have come about through the creation of "word pictures" based on photographs or other pictures that evoke a memory, feeling, or image. In order to create a poem that resembles a "still" from a movie, perhaps one shot from a unique angle, students concentrate on finding one striking element in the picture. They then draw a circle in the middle of a blank page in their logs and create a "web" of as many associated, descriptive words that they can think of. Some prompts you might give to start the process include:

- What movements, thoughts, people, things, and/or elements of nature do you observe?
- What is the one element of the picture that most strikes you?
- Where is this item or event?
- What does it remind you of?
- How does this picture make you feel?
- What mood does this picture convey?

Students freeze the image and add any last words that will capture it. Taking all the words and phrases they have written, students cut them out and begin to organize them into an "image" poem. They arrange and rearrange the words and add new words or phrases until they are satisfied with the order. Students can share their work with a partner so that they can discuss further revisions. When all students are satisfied with their "poem," they can paste the revised copy in their logs.

Found Poems

Even the most reluctant writers get involved in creating "found poetry" because, as Miranda once said, "All I do is borrow the words and arrange them!" This activity is most effective when students work with a partner. Together, they begin by generating a list of recent topics they find exciting, worrisome, or upsetting, scouring magazines and newspapers if necessary. When they have decided on a topic, the partners cut out words from magazines and newspapers that are related to their topic and/or are needed for the structure of their poem. Once the words are on the page, they can be arranged and rearranged, deleted, and added to.

A bulletin board display is a most effective way to showcase found poetry. The variety will be outstanding, as will some of the poems.

Bringing it All Together: Evaluation Activities

Drawing on their poetry experiences to create a meaningful end product that can be shared with others is a satisfying way for students to conclude this unit. The following suggestions are only some of the numerous activities students can choose to complete. The activities range from individual works through class projects.

1. Publish a class poetry magazine. All students contribute two or three favorite poems before joining either the editorial staff (groups, orders the poems) or the production staff (illustrates, designs, binds).
2. Present, in small groups, a poetry reading session that includes both published and unpublished poems organized around a theme. Readings can include solo, paired, and choral readings. A script introduces and links each of the poems.
3. Present a poem by reading it aloud. Accompany the reading with complementary slides, music, and movement.
4. Create an anthology of at least 15 puzzle poems.
5. Publish a class poetry book that focuses on a theme and that includes both published and unpublished poems. Editorial and production processes can follow those outlined in Activity #1.
6. Compile poems on one theme. A collage can be created that makes a statement about the poems included in the collection, and a preface can be written that outlines the selection process.

CHAPTER FIVE

"The Play's the Thing" — Building Meaning Through Performance

I can't help thinking about my own experiences in "studying" drama, which, of course, was synonymous with Shakespeare. The "study" consisted of reading scenes of a play for homework and then listening to the teacher explain, define, and interpret what we had read. Naturally we recorded these explanations and interpretations because we knew that we would be expected to call on them when answering quizzes and writing essays. For some unknown reason, I still developed a deep and abiding love for Shakespeare. Perhaps it came from my personal (subversive) connections with the characters: love-at-first-sight Juliet, pure and innocent Desdemona, patently evil Iago, procrastinating Hamlet, or defiant and rebellious Kate.

When I began teaching, I assumed that Shakespeare would be resisted or at best tolerated, and that only at my insistence. I was wrong in this assumption — my students enjoyed Shakespeare in spite of my teaching and their past experience. Their positive reaction may have been due to the fact that I believed plays were meant to be acted and that students would participate as either actors or audience. In addition, I used recordings and films to bring performances to life. I was, to be frank, taken aback by their responses. Krista, who had been only marginally interested in English all year, came to me in February as we were about to begin "Romeo and Juliet" and brashly announced, "I've been waiting for this all year!" Willie, Ed's classmate, came to me after class one day and said sheepishly, "Do you think I could borrow the Romeo and Juliet movie for the weekend? I really want my boyfriend and parents to see it." The essence of drama had captured them!

Bringing Drama Alive

I try to do two plays a year — one modern and one Shakespearean drama. We begin with the modern play since the language and theme of many such plays are accessible to the students. An overview of the process I employ is found on page 93. Students then undertake "Romeo and Juliet." This chapter comprises a detailed outline of the process I use when working with the play, and includes devices such as surveys that help students relate the theme of the play to personal attitudes and experience. Through writing, reflecting, and discussing, students come to understand the universality and timelessness of Shakespeare's plays.

Assessment and Evaluation Criteria for the Drama Unit

The following criteria, discussed with students at the beginning of the unit, provide a basis for discussion and writing about learning. I read students' logs, observe their participation in discussions and group work, and watch their performance in order to assess and evaluate their ability to:

- represent ideas and feelings,
- display commitment and engagement in drama,
- accept and develop a role through active involvement,
- identify with the role of a character,
- explore a character through writing in a log,
- understand the characters in a drama,
- select, shape, and present ideas and feelings,
- contribute, receive, and modify meanings,
- reveal and share insights,
- question concepts within a drama,
- link characters and problems to personal life and experience,
- share work in progress,
- understand the drama genre,
- demonstrate growth in and appreciation for the drama form,
- actively question and explore a drama,
- appreciate diverse drama forms,
- participate as a thoughtful and responsive audience member.

Given the nature of this unit, I adjust the distribution of marks as follows:

Reading response logs: 30
Final product: 20
Contributions to group, class discussions: 50

When assigning this expanded discussion and group-work mark, I consider students' involvement in small- and large-group situations, as well as their involvement with roles they assume as a group member in the course of presenting a play.

The final product mark is reduced since much of its focus rests with the process leading to the performance and the extensive group work this entails.

While the logs also generate a smaller portion of the final mark than is typical, their importance here is no less than in previous units. In fact, the drama unit offers an ideal opportunity to introduce students to new uses for their logs, including that of tracking a character. I divide the evaluation of the logs into two separate, equal marks: one for regular log work, and one for tracking a character. Here is a brief overview of this activity.

Students select one character that they would like to explore. The character does not have to play a major role in the drama nor do students have to portray the character in a performance. Each day, students record their responses to the character and the events that affect him or her. As the play progresses, students write in the voice of the character and interpret events from his or her viewpoint. In the instance where a student has selected a minor character, she or he can write "meanwhile" episodes that explore the character's actions and reactions while "offstage." By the play's end, students will have insight into the character's personality and the role played in the drama. This insight is of a different nature than that gleaned by performing in the role of a character since the student will, in essence, observe the character and the forces that motivate him or her. This unbiased observation helps students to understand why the playwright included the role of the character and how she or he contributed to the play's development and outcome.

A FIVE-STAGE MODEL FOR WORKING WITH MODERN PLAYS

Introducing the Play

Teacher
- provides "entry" prompt (e.g., title, picture, related problem)
- shares related resources (e.g., books, films) if possible
- explains reading, rehearsing, and performing processes, schedules
- explains 5-step process for acts
1. read the act in role in groups
2. respond in log to characters/ events/personal reactions after each reading
3. share responses with group
4. share responses with whole class
5. add new info, reflections to log
- hands out copies of play

Students
- respond to entry prompt in log
- form small groups of 4 to 5 members

Exploring the Play

Teacher
- circulates among groups, offers assistance when necessary

Students
- repeat 5-step process for each act

Rehearsing the Play

Teacher
- divides class according to acts
- assigns acts to be rehearsed, performed
- decides, with students, intended audience
- acts as director — keeps groups in sync

Students
- assign roles
- decide, with teacher, intended audience
- set group schedule for rehearsals
- write "Who am I?" log entries of characters they are portraying

Performing the Play

Teacher
- sets schedule, with students, for dress rehearsals
- provides feedback to rehearsing group
- observes individual/group performances

Students
- set schedule, with teacher, for dress rehearsals
- perform 5-minute rehearsal
- provide feedback to rehearsing group
- present play

Reflecting on the Play

Teacher
- circulates among small groups

Students
- complete 20-minute freewrite on play experiences
- share freewrite with members of original small group

"Romeo and Juliet"

I usually try to time the production of this play so that it takes place in February, a salute to Valentine's Day. While everyone recognizes the names of the doomed characters Romeo and Juliet, far fewer know of the finer parts of the play's plot: family feuds, an arranged marriage, scheming, wedding preparations with a different groom, networking that fails so tragically, and the brief time span of the play.

I often use the opinionnaire on the next page as an introduction to the play and it always generates the same results. Students love to talk about relationships and feel strongly about their views. They record their answers, scribbling reasons below the statements if they like. When they have finished, students discuss the opinionnaire in small groups. Discussion of some statements results in a genuine debate — students' feelings and reasons for these feelings are important to them. There is little need for me to participate in the discussions since students emit enough steam to keep the talk moving at a fast pace! I do ask them to paste the opinionnaire in their logs since they will refer to it again at the end of the first run-through of the play.

Introducing the Play: The Reading Response Log

Almost all students know the names of Romeo and Juliet and have some idea of the basic story — the two meet, fall in love, and die. I ask them to record in their logs what they know of "Romeo and Juliet" by generating a word cache — a collection of related words and phrases that students record as quickly as possible within a three- to five-minute time frame.

Together, we list the words on a chart. Students tell me that it's about "love and romance," "doomed love," and will sometimes quote, "Romeo, Romeo, wherefore art thou Romeo?" that suggests that Juliet doesn't know *where* Romeo is, rather than *who* he is! Students know that Shakespeare wrote the script.

I tell the students that as the actors and directors of this play we will take part in a number of activities: reading aloud the scenes; practising reading; writing and talking about each scene; watching the film "Romeo and Juliet"; and listening to music. Because male roles predominate, I encourage girls to take on any male role they'd like. We become, at this time, a Shakespearean acting company. I divide the study of the play into three phases: reading aloud, rehearsals, and performance.

THE TRUE LOVE OPINIONNAIRE

Directions: Read each of the following statements. Write **A** if you agree, **D** if you disagree. Think about the reasons for your answer and record them if you like.

____ 1. If you really care for someone, there is nothing wrong with doing whatever you have to do, even lying, to get the person to love you.

____ 2. If you are really in love, the longer you and your partner are together, the stronger your love grows.

____ 3. True love is worth dying for if necessary.

____ 4. True lovers should never flirt with other people of the opposite sex.

____ 5. Lovers are always happy.

____ 6. It is never right to scheme just to get someone you like to go out with you.

____ 7. It is unwise to go against parental wishes in choosing a marriage partner.

____ 8. True lovers should spend as much time together as possible.

____ 9. "Love at first sight" is enough to justify getting married immediately.

____ 10. If you are really in love, physical appearance does not matter.

____ 11. Love never happens suddenly. It always needs time to grow.

____ 12. It is never right to go out with someone just because she or he is popular.

____ 13. Physical attraction must always come before true love.

____ 14. If you are really in love, family connections or social standing is not important.

Reading Aloud

The First Read Aloud

For the first phase, I post a schedule outlining the days that will be devoted to reading aloud each act. For each scene, I list the characters, and leave a space for students to sign up. Act I, for instance, has 31 speaking parts (not including revelers and citizens) so each member must sign up for at least one part. [Act I: Scene 1 — 10 characters: Sampson, Gregory, Benvolio, Tybalt, Capulet, Lady Capulet, Montague, Lady Montague, Prince, Romeo]

I have used the following resources to help students understand the introduction to the play: a model of the Globe Theatre (helps students to visualize how the play was first produced), a tape of Prokofiev's "Romeo and Juliet" (play during reading of opening scene), and the Zeffirelli film version of the play (helps students visualize the opening, the Ball, the balcony scene, the final scene). While there are others available, I try to limit the number of resources students are exposed to in order to keep the acting company "on track."

The Chronolog

A chronolog is a time chart that records the details of the play: the time, place, and event. Because "Romeo and Juliet" occurs in a brief time span, the chronolog helps students to see how events are ordered and in what time frame they occur. Students devote a page in their log for the entering of "daily data" that emerges as they read the play.

THE CHRONOLOG		
Time	Place	Event
Early Sunday Morning	Market Place Verona, Italy	A fight between servants and members of the two houses: Montague & Capulet

New Roles for the Reading Response Log

The log takes a few turns here. I use it for the first part of the study as a "triple-entry notebook" and later, during the rehearsal phase, as a "prompt book." In both instances, students use the logs to stay tuned to the play and as a vehicle for discussion.

As a triple-entry notebook, the log becomes a place for summarizing what happens in the scenes and generating a response to the reading through reactions, questions, and predictions. The easiest format to follow is to use a left page for the summary, and a right page for the response. An alternative is to use the top part of a page for the summary, and the bottom part of a page for the response. The following questions help some students get started:

- How do you respond to this?
- What struck you about this section?
- What alternatives do the characters have at this point?
- What would you do in this circumstance? Why?
- What advice would you give to _____? Why?
- What kind of actions/feelings dominate this section?
- What have you learned that you didn't know before?
- Have you heard of a similar situation in real life?
- How do you visualize this section?

The third component of the triple-entry notebook comprises the responses of others to the writing, which are made in the small-group discussions (marginal jottings). This keeps the process interactive and dynamic.

Sharif, a 14-year-old Grade 9 student, wrote the following response to the first section of "Romeo and Juliet."

> I think that it is a bit odd that Romeo and Juliet are in each other's arms and saying that their lives are not worth living without each other after they had only met each other for the first time a few minutes ago.
>
> After Romeo is discovered gatecrashing Capulet's party why is he not thrown out immediately? Instead he is allowed to stay and chat up Capulet's only daughter. What happens to Paris who was supposed to be introduced to Juliet? Surely Lady Capulet whose idea it was in the first place would make more of an effort.

I can't help thinking that if there was no Tybalt the rela-
tions between the Montague and Capulet families would be a
good deal better. Also Tybalt's powers of perception must be
truly brilliant to recognize a Montague underneath a mask
just by his voice. Also another great disappearance — what
happened to Rosaline? Did she find true love elsewhere?
Up until Act 2 Scene 2 the Nurse was the most prominent
character. The nurse is a very good character to have around
as she tends to throw a little more light on the more complicated situations.
 I think that the more prologues the better, it is a very good
idea to have one at the start of each act.

Into the Script: A Choral Reading of the Prologue

We open the reading of the play with a choral reading of the prologue. (I prepare it as an overhead so that all can see it.) Phrases
are spaced to suggest pauses between the responses. Everyone
sits and forms a circle on the floor. For the first round, one
students reads the first phrase, the reader beside him or her the
second, and so on until we have read the entire prologue. Then
I divide the class in half or into male/female sections. Students
sit in a circle facing one another, and each half reads one portion:

Two households,	both alike in dignity
(In fair Verona	where we lay our scene),
From ancient grudge	break to new mutiny,
Where civil blood	makes civil hands unclean.
From forth the fatal loins	of these two foes
A pair of star-crossed lovers	take their life;
Whose misadventured	piteous overthrows
Doth with their death	bury their parents' strife.
The fearful passage	of their death-marked love
And the continuance	of their parents' rage,
Which, but their children's end	naught could remove,
Is now the two hours' traffic	of our stage;
The which, if you	with patient ears attend,
What here shall miss,	our toils shall strive to mend.

In the circle, students discuss the events. What do they hear
about? What words could they add to their Romeo and Juliet word
cache? They suggest some additional words and phrases:
grudge/foes/star-crossed lovers/overthrows/fearful/death-marked
love. Students have a sense of what's to come.

Introducing Act I, Scene 1: The Zeffirelli Film

Of the many ways I have introduced this play, I have found show-ing Zeffirelli's "Romeo and Juliet" to be the most effective. Without the benefit of viewing this film, students tend to miss the initial puns and the visual picture of the market and the fights — it's a wonderful assisted invitation into the play.

After watching the first part of the film, students can reflect in their logs on what they have seen. Sometimes I suggest starters, though they don't often use them:

- What is the situation so far?
- Where do you think this will lead?
- Whose side are you on? Why?
- What do you wonder about?
- What do you predict?
- What feelings emerge in this section?
- What event or character did you find striking?

When they have finished, we discuss as a class what they have learned from watching this portion of the film — who they have met, the type of characters they are, and what will result from this scenario.

Ready to Read

From this point, students begin the class with the assigned scenes for the day. A large-group discussion of how the actors read and what needs to be considered for the performance is also held. Actors identify trouble spots and where they would benefit from directorial suggestions. Depending on the difficulty of the scene, the class may read through it a second time.

During each class, students use the log as a triple-entry notebook. They (1) fill in the chronolog, (2) respond to the scenes presented, and (3) respond to entries in other people's logs. In other words, they connect to the script through reading, writing, talking, and listening as they move through the play.

At the end of Act I, students begin to think seriously about the notion of love and how differently not only members of our class feel (given the discussion of the opinionnaire), but also how different members of the cast feel. The "Love Connection" on the next page helps students to identify the competing visions of love cast in the play. Working with a partner, students read through the script until they are able to define, albeit briefly, the vision of love to which each character adheres. They begin by listing words and phrases they have noted about each character and how they think she or he might feel about love. Partners take turns reading each of the text's citations aloud before summarizing what they have found.

THE LOVE CONNECTION

Read the lines listed for each of the following characters. In the first column, write the lines as they appear in the play. Think about your impression of each character you've developed so far, then draw some conclusions about each line or set of lines. What insights do they give into each character's experiences with and attitudes toward love and marriage? Jot down these insights in the third column.

Character	Line	Conclusions
Romeo	1.1.195-199	
Benvolio	1.1.224, 235, 1.2.47-48	
Paris	1.2.12	
Capulet	1.2.13, 1.2.16-17	
Juliet	1.3.71, 1.3.98-100	
Lady Capulet	1.3.75-79	
Nurse	1.3.101	
Mercutio	1.4.27	

The discussions that follow inevitably include arranged marriages, love-at-first-sight, choosing one's path, loving a partner more than parents, and so on.

The Prologue

As in Act I, the next prologue can be read in a similar fashion.

Now old desire doth in his deathbed lie,
and young affection gapes to be his heir
That fair for which love groaned for and would die,
With tender Juliet matched, is now not fair.
Now Romeo is beloved and loves again,
Alike bewitched by the charm of looks,
But to his foe supposed he must complain,
And she steal love's sweet bait from fearful hooks.
Being held a foe, he may not have access
To breathe such vows as lovers use to swear,
And she as much in love, her means much less
To meet her new beloved anywhere.
But passion lends them power, time means, to meet,
Tempering extremities with extreme sweet.

As the readings progress, actors add to their triple-entry notebook, chronolog, and group discussions. They view parts of the film or listen to taped recordings of challenging scenes. The amount of secondary resources will vary (I add them as I see fit).

In small groups of four or five, students create a sociogram at the end of the first reading of the play. This helps them to remember the characters and the family to which they belong.

A SOCIOGRAM

Your group's task is to design a sociogram of the main characters in "Romeo and Juliet," which you will present to the rest of the class. To complete this assignment, you will need four different-colored pens and a blank sheet of paper.

Design your sociogram to include the following characters:

Paris	Benvolio	Lady Montague
Montague	Tybalt	Lady Capulet
Capulet	Balthasar	Juliet
Nurse	Romeo	Mercutio
Sampson	Gregory	Friar Laurence

When you have finished the sociogram, include a key at the bottom of the page that indicates to readers how they should interpret the lines and colors.

Finally, pick any two-character relationship and, using your sociogram as a reference, describe the relationship in your log.

Reviewing the True Love Opinionnaire

Working with the True Love Opinionnaire is a delightful activity to engage in at this point. Students form five small groups, with each group assuming the role of one of the following characters from the play: Romeo, Juliet, Nurse, Paris, and Capulet. Groups answer each statement from the perspective of their character and present findings to members of the other groups who can question or challenge their selection.

Reviewing the Chronolog

One of the more surprising elements of this play is its time frame. By recording all the times for each event (see page 96), students recognize the enormity of what has happened. We use the topic of "whirlwind romances" as a basis for a class discussion. How reasonable is such a romance? Where will it lead? What would the students do in Romeo or Juliet's position? What advice would they give the lovers?

Rehearsing the Play

I begin rehearsals by posting a schedule for rehearsal time, and the roles involved in each scene. I generally allow four to five classes for rehearsals and two classes for performance. Members sign up for a scene and at least one of the play's 31 roles (given this number, some students will have to assume the roles of two characters). Acting groups are formed on the basis of which scenes students have chosen. All students receive a copy of the scenes in which they are participating. They can paste the scenes in their log so that it now serves as a prompt book. The following represent the major scenes that my students perform.

Act I, Scene 3, Lines 69-99: Nurse, Juliet, Lady Capulet
(Lady Capulet tells Juliet of her proposed marriage to Paris)

Act I, Scene 5, Lines 94-145: Romeo, Juliet, Nurse
(Romeo and Juliet meet at the feast given by Juliet's parents)

Act II, Scene 2, Lines 1-190: Romeo and Juliet
(complete scene, balcony)

Act III, Scene 1, Lines 1-202: Romeo, Tybalt, Benvolio, Mercutio, Prince
(complete scene, fight in which Mercutio and Tybalt are killed)

Act IV, Scene 1, Lines 44-125: Friar Laurence and Juliet
(Friar Laurence comes up with a plan to make Juliet appear dead)

Act IV, Scene 5, Lines 1-95: Nurse, Lady Capulet, Capulet, Friar Laurence
(Juliet is found "dead": the marriage plans become funeral arrangements)

Act V, Scene 1, Lines 1-57: Balthasar and Romeo
(Romeo learns of Juliet's "death")

Act V, Scene 3, Lines 1-309: Balthasar, Romeo, Paris, Paris' page, Capulet, Lady Capulet, Prince, Friar Laurence, Night Watchman, Montague
(complete scene, final where Romeo kills Paris, Romeo kills himself, Juliet kills herself, bodies are found, Friar Laurence tells the full story, families are reconciled)

As a daily part of each class, I schedule a large chunk of class time for rehearsal. This is followed by small-group discussions where we plan for the next rehearsal and ensure that all members are memorizing their lines. At the end of each class, we have a whole-group discussion on the rehearsal process and have demonstrations where students can get feedback on their scenes. Throughout the rehearsal period, I make myself available to each group, offer assistance, and monitor members' progress. We usually end up discussing the meaning of a line or deciding how a line should be spoken. The actors are usually quite eager to prepare for the performance.

The Reading Response Log and Rehearsals

Along with memorizing lines, keeping a record of decisions regarding how lines are to be delivered, and how characters are to move, I ask students to keep a personal journal on their character. Who is she or he? How does she or he behave? How do other characters react to him or her? How does their character speak to and respond to others? These entries can be discussed in the acting groups so that students are clear about their characters and how they interact with others in the scene.

Performing the Play

The big day finally arrives. It is sometimes helpful to have one actor provide a one- or two-line introduction (e.g., Act I, Scene 3: Lady Capulet tells Juliet of her proposed marriage to Paris). The drama can then begin.

At the end of each day, the whole class meets in a circle. The actors describe their roles and the characters they played. Audience members can then ask the actors questions about scene presentation or about the characters portrayed. This keeps the students' attention on the play.

Bringing It All Together: Evaluation Activities

These activities can be completed by individuals, by pairs of students, or by small groups of students. (I generally let students select their own activity and work situation). Students can also devise an activity if they are not satisfied with the choices presented here. When everyone has finished, the class holds a "Romeo and Juliet Revisiting Feast" where the products of the activities are displayed or performed for the class.

1. Create a scene from a "What if..." standpoint, for example: What would have happened if Juliet had not died?
2. Write an article for an entertainment magazine (e.g., *People, Hello*) that outlines the saga of Romeo and Juliet's romance, including quotes from family members and friends and "photos" (illustrations).
3. Host a talk show where one student role plays the host, other students role play the guests (e.g., Romeo, Juliet, Lady Capulet).
4. Publish a "Town Crier" newspaper that includes lead stories, as well as fashion, art, theatre, classified, and society pages that reflect Romeo and Juliet's Verona.
5. Create a mural of the most striking scene in the play.
6. Make an illustrated A-B-C book that includes one word from or related to the play for each letter of the alphabet. Each word should be used in a sentence about the play.
7. Construct props needed to stage one scene in the play.

CHAPTER SIX

The Stories of Our Lives — An Integrated Theme

Ed's school experiences had given him a genuine depth of understanding and identity when he encountered the world of black Rev. Kumalo in *Cry, the Beloved Country*. Something stirred inside him and he responded in kind in his log. His peers joined him. They faced a world that no longer believed in their ability to be genuine partners in an academic learning community — they were excluded from the club. They understood the pain evident in the novel. Empathy was evident in Willie's log: *I feel sorry for Rev. Kumalo because ever since he came to Johannesburg, all the news he got was bad news. And he seems like he becomes a year older every day. It sounds like his appearance has changed. In the beginning he sounded like a strong man but now he's beginning to turn into an old man because he has had such a rough time and so many worries.*

When Ed and his peers had prepared their own auto-biographies, the stories and journeys of their lives, they were ready to read narratives and meet women and men of other cultures, languages, and immigration experiences in a mosaic of genres and response strategies. They responded eagerly and with compassion.

In this chapter, we draw on the response strategies and genres studies focussed on in the preceding chapters — short stories, novels, poetry, and drama — and organize them into an integrated theme exploring cultures.

Through the literature explored in this theme, students develop some understanding of the nature of culture and how cultural context shapes the way we live and who we become. They begin by thinking about their own lives and who they are as contemporary teenagers, and see how cultural influences contribute to their tastes, customs, values, and beliefs. This involves consideration of issues and events that shape their ethnic and cultural heritage including, for many, the immigrant experience. Students then explore other cultures. In small groups, they compare, contrast, and explain the lives of people who live in cultures other than their own.

Literature allows us to enter into the lives and feelings of others in ways that we cannot in everyday life. Response to literature necessarily involves empathy and understanding of characters and the predicaments they face. One of the outcomes of this theme is a deepening understanding of the nature of our own responses. The way we respond to a text is influenced by the value systems we hold and that have been shaped by our cultural background, as well as by our personal experiences. Inevitably, we all see a text through a personal set of cultural lenses. As readers, students who develop an increased understanding of the cultural contexts that have formed their value and belief systems are more likely to see their responses to text as culturally determined.

I developed this chapter as an attempt to address some of these issues with students and to provide an example of how a theme can be explored in the classroom. Reflective of its topic, this model is most efficient when it is a joint project between English teachers and history teachers.

Themes are a way of organizing curriculum so that students may employ individual skills in the pursuit of a common idea using a variety of materials and approaches to the learning. Themes are particularly successful in mixed-ability classrooms where students with a range of experience and knowledge can be accommodated. Objectives, assignments, outcomes, and evaluation can be modified to meet the needs of the learners within a framework of investigation that links everyone's work.

There are numerous advantages to this type of curriculum organization: it capitalizes on students' growing competencies and independence; it allows the students and ourselves the chance to apply previously learned strategies to explore a main idea through a variety of genres; it combines curriculum goals of several disciplines, allowing us to use the expertise and resources of our fellow teachers; and it integrates a number of genres so that students experience the holistic nature of learning. Through the study of short stories, novels, poetry, plays, newspapers, films, videos, pictures, maps, and so on, students are encouraged to make connections and see relationships in a rich and diversified literary context. By representing the learning using a variety of genres and meaningful activities, all students will have frequent opportunities for success.

Why choose this theme? What are the learning outcomes that may result? When students study their own culture they feel an increased sense of their own value and worth. Through the study and sharing of cultures in our classroom, we enhance the self-esteem of individuals and encourage tolerance. Developing empathy and understanding of other cultures can only lead to a happier environment in a diverse society.

An Introduction to the Theme

A first requirement of this chapter is to define the term "culture." We begin this exploration by holding a whole-class discussion where students can share what they believe is the meaning of the term. During this process, I record their definitions on the board or a chart. When students have exhausted their supply of definitions, we do a 10-minute freewrite where they write about culture in their home, their school, and their community. At the end of the freewrite, students find a partner. Together, they write a definition of culture that expresses both partners' viewpoints. As a large group, we compare the definitions arrived at when working with a partner with those given at the beginning of the class. Students then choose one definition that they think best captures the meaning of culture.

Depending on the class's grasp of the concept, I sometimes share Tiedt and Tiedt's comprehensive definition: "Culture is a totality of values, beliefs, and behaviours common to a large group of people. A culture may include shared language and folklore, ideas and thinking patterns, communication styles — the "truth" accepted by members of the group" (1990, p. 10). We discuss how these collective beliefs, values, customs, and traditions provide members of a culture with a shared sense of identity. Within a multicultural society, students begin to see that members may belong to more than one cultural group while for immigrants, there will be differences between members of the same family based on generation and length of time spent in the new country.

Exploring Culture Through Autobiographical Scrapbooks

Many schools today comprise a diverse student population that is representative of all parts of the world. Such diversity brings a wealth of cultural experience that must be valued and reflected in the content we explore. As schools can be considered a microcosm of the society in which they are situated, they reflect in part Marshall McLuhan's concept of the world becoming a global village. Today's students are witness to and participants of this global transformation. While this is an important issue for everyone, it is of particular relevance to the young since it is they who will chart the progress of the next century.

This activity provides students with a unique opportunity to observe the major role that culture plays in family traditions, customs, and ways of communicating. Interviews with family members, and data in the form of letters, artifacts, and folklore, for example, help students to define their culture and its role in their life. When shared with peers who have engaged in similar explorations, students are provided with the chance to appreciate their culture and that of others, and to witness first-hand the value and benefits of living in a cultural mosaic.

Assessment and Evaluation Criteria for the Autobiographical Scrapbook

I discuss with the students that their autobiographical scrapbooks will be marked out of 50. Of these 50 marks, 20 marks will be allotted to their log and the gathering of materials (the process). Together, we review the criteria that I will look for in their logs:

- being aware of and appreciating personal culture, values, habits, and celebrations,
- accepting differences among cultural groups,
- understanding effects of stereotyping and racism,
- appreciating literature as a cultural artifact,
- willingness to learn about other cultures through literature,
- recognizing and accepting differences and similarities of cultures other than one's own,
- appreciating mores and customs of other cultures,
- participating in other cultural forms of response to literature,
- responding reflectively to literature in the log,

- using the log to discuss texts,
- demonstrating breadth in reading of literature from other cultures,
- seeking to understand literature through logs and discussions,
- openly expressing views of literature in group discussions,
- drawing links between literature and personal experiences,
- empathizing with characters presented in the literature.

During the research or gathering stage of the project, assessment can be done by noting the completion of various components of the process. Setting up a schedule of events helps to track the learning and keeps students accountable for the process as it evolves. Some suggestions include: gathering personal writing, letters, pictures, and family stories, and creating family trees. It can also be done in the publication "stages" of the scrapbook (e.g., proposal, initial culling of material).

Whatever you decide, alert students to the deadlines before the process begins. All students are expected to participate and are assessed on the degree of their participation. Keeping a class list and checking off a student's name when she or he finishes assignments is an efficient way to monitor progress.

The scrapbook will be marked out of 30 (the product). Students write a one-page outline of their scrapbook followed by a proposal. In a conference, we discuss the proposal and agree on how the mark will be broken down according to the criteria discussed.

At the end of the project, I ask the students to submit a self-evaluation using this criteria. Final marks are determined through the combination of the student's evaluation and my evaluation. In addition to meeting the criteria listed in the proposal, the scrapbooks are evaluated for:

- content (organization, clarity, detail, relevance, originality),
- mechanics (neatness, grammar, spelling and punctuation).

In evaluating these works, it is important to respect their personal nature. The scrapbook is a document that students can take pride in and share with others. With this in mind, I write my comments on separate pieces of paper so that the document is not marred.

Opening the Reading Response Log

In this activity, the log serves two functions: (1) as a repository of responses to material students read in the course of the activity, and (2) as a warehouse of personal writing. In essence, the log will comprise all material generated throughout the duration of the activity.

Students can begin their work with this activity by engaging in a 10-minute freewrite that sets the stage for the work to come. Here are some suggested journal prompts to stimulate free writing.

- Who are you today? What has brought you to this point?
- What makes you tick?
- Who is the most important person in your life? Why?
- Who has influenced you as a role model?
- Who has helped you? How did she or he help you?
- What type of person do you admire? What type of person do you dislike? Why?
- What are your ambitions in life?
- What are your hopes and dreams? What would you love to do or be if only you could?
- How do you like to spend your free time?
- Do you work outside of school? What sort of work do you do?
- What special occasions does your family celebrate?
- What are your parents' or grandparents' origins?
- What languages are spoken in your family?
- Retell a personal story based on something that happened to your family. This might be a story you heard or it might be an event you experienced.
- What special foods are eaten in your family? When are they eaten? Does your family have rituals that involve food? If yes, what do the rituals represent?
- What sayings or proverbs are used in your family? What do they mean?
- What family traditions are celebrated in your family on a daily, weekly, or yearly basis?
- Does your family possess a special object or artifact? What significance does the piece hold? Where does it come from? How did it come to be in your family?

A Six-Stage Process of Exploration

Once students have completed their freewrite, they are ready to embark on the creation of their scrapbook. This activity comprises the following six stages:

Stage One: Defining Criteria for Success
Stage Two: Creating a One-Page Outline and a Proposal
Stage Three: Collecting Information
Stage Four: Selecting Material for Publication
Stage Five: Publishing the Scrapbook
Stage Six: Sharing with an Audience

Stage One: Defining Criteria for Success

Typically, I like to treat this stage in a whole-class situation. This allows students the opportunity to share their experiences of reading autobiographical literature. They can discuss specific books and authors with which they are familiar, and can identify ways in which these books differ from fiction and other content texts.

Suggested titles that can be considered strong examples of this genre are listed below. Students who have had limited exposure to autobiographical writing may want to read parts or all of one or more of these books before they begin their work. Autobiographical writing provides students with a model of ways in which writers communicate a sense of who they are, an important component of their work in this theme. Awareness of the organization and style of a memoir helps students with this activity.

I Know Why the Caged Bird Sings by Maya Angelou. Bantam Books: New York, NY, 1969.

The Education of Little Tree by Forest Carter. University of New Mexico Press: Alberquerque, NM, 1986.

Homesick: My Own Story by Jean Fritz. Putnam Publishing Group: New York, NY, 1982.

Fierce Attachments: A Memoir by Vivian Gornic. Farrar, Straus & Giroux: New York, NY, 1987.

Little by Little: A Writer's Education by Jean Little. Penguin Books of Canada: Toronto, ON, 1987.

As a class, we discuss the goal of the activity: to create a scrapbook that is not so much a chronicle of events, places, and achievements as it is a collage of people, places, and ideas that have influenced and shaped them as people. Students' scrapbooks can include personal journal entries, letters to family members, interviews with family members, photographs, drawings, magazine clippings, quotes, stories, poems, family histories, and memoirs. The end result of the activity is the creation of a document that reflects the students and that, when shared, informs others of important facets of their culture.

Stage Two: Creating a One-Page Outline and a Proposal

Students begin this stage by writing a one-page proposal that outlines the scope of their project. This activity is useful for several purposes: it helps each student to define the direction of his or her scrapbook, and it provides a basis for a teacher-student conference. Together, we review the outline, noting any areas that might be problematic, and brainstorm for other resources available to the student that might prove beneficial to the final outcome of the project. When both the student and I are satisfied that the outline is representative of his or her goals, she or he expands the outline and creates a proposal. Included here are two samples of student proposals for this activity.

1. Jennifer's Proposal
a) Ten family photographs, each with a paragraph outlining who is in the photo, what they are doing, and how the photo illustrates something significant about the history of my family.
b) An interview with my grandmother on the subject of life in Canada when she was a girl. I will tape and transcribe the interview so it can be included in my scrapbook.
c) A reflection on the interview that answers these questions: What did I learn about my grandmother as a person? What did I learn about her life that surprised or interested me the most? What are the biggest differences between her life and my life?
d) Two journal entries, done in class in response to journal prompts, edited and revised.

In drawing up the contract, Jennifer and I decide that the photo essay and the interview and reflections on her grandmother's life will each be worth 10 marks. The two journal entries will each be worth five marks.

2. Manraaj's Proposal

a) An account of the major religious festivals in the Sikh calendar. For each festival, I will outline the importance of the celebration and its significance in the belief system of Sikhism. I will also describe how my family celebrates the festival. This essay will be illustrated with drawings and quotations in Hindi (Manraaj's first language) and with family photographs.

b) An interview with a local politician from the Sikh community who is a member of my family. I will ask him the following questions: What are the most important issues facing members of your constituency? Are there differences between political life here and politics in India? What are they? What are the problems faced by members of our Sikh community? Are they the same as problems faced by other communities or are there specific differences?

c) I will include two edited journal entries written in class.

Manraaj and I agree that the photo essay on Sikhism will take the largest chunk of time and will involve the most research. As a result, it will be marked out of 15. The transcript of the interview and the two journal entries will be worth five marks each.

Stage Three: Collecting Information

The following methods represent ways in which students can gather material to help them explore their cultural roots.

1. Students select a family member they would like to interview. Given the nature of the task, it is best if they interview an older member of the family, for example, a parent, aunt or uncle, or grandparent. Before they start the interview, students need to determine the type of information they are seeking. To help them draft their interview, I provide example of prompts they may use:

- Tell me about your first day at school.
- What did you want to be when you grew up?
- What are your most memorable life experiences?
- What is the most important thing that has ever happened to you?
- What are the religious influences in your life?
- What is your favorite book/story/play/piece of music?
- What cultural traditions are most important to you?
- Tell me about family traditions or celebrations that you most value.

Students in my classes have found that interviewing a family member can hold some surprising results, and makes them aware of how we often operate under preconceived notions. Students record their interview in their logs, later transcribing it for their scrapbooks. (If possible, students can videotape their interview.) If they wish, they can include photographs or other artifacts. The interview often forms the basis for the scrapbook; other material gathered by the students tends to serve as supplementary information.

2. Students, with the permission of family members, can collect letters that describe experiences and events that have shaped the lives of family members. Subjects of the letters can include, as examples, an account of a wedding, a birthday party, a celebration, a war story, or news from relatives and friends in other parts of the world.

3. Weddings, funerals, birthdays, anniversaries, reunions, and other family celebrations offer students a rich source of stories. They can describe in their logs one such event that they have attended. Photos from the event provide a strong visual element to their storytelling.

4. Every family has stories. Some are funny, some sad, some exciting, and some poignant. Grandparents and other relatives provide a rich source of stories from a family's history. Students can ask a family member to tell a favorite story. If possible, students should tape the storytelling to best capture its language and intonation. They can later transcribe the tape, or write the story in their own words in their logs.

5. Students can represent their family origins by creating a family tree. They can embellish it by adding the country of birth to each of the generations represented and include photographs of family members.

6. Many families pass stories from one generation to the next. Students can summarize in their log folktales they have heard told in their family. If they have trouble recalling folktales, they can ask a family member for help or check with a librarian for folktales from their culture. From these summaries, students choose a favorite tale and retell it in their own words.

Stage Four: Selecting Material for Publication

At this point, students' logs comprise a wealth of material including jottings, memories, ideas, responses to literature, webs, transcripts, and notes. They are now ready to begin culling material for inclusion in their scrapbook. Students must reread their material carefully, noting ideas that stand out from the others, and themes that are repeated or have particular significance. These items form the cornerstones of the scrapbooks.

Students need to determine the writing that most reflects who they are and what they believe. Entries are reworked, reflected on, revisited, and crafted into short stories, personal memoirs, essays, plays, or poems. A note may become a poem; a paragraph in the log, a short story. Other pieces, such as interviews, may be directly transcribed and placed in the scrapbook.

I usually allow two to three class periods for this stage of the scrapbook. Students need time to reread, rethink, and in many cases reshape their work so that their final product is reflective of their culture, their family, and ultimately themselves.

Although editorial decisions rest in the hands of writers, I have found that supportive responses and questions on my part during conferences are usually appreciated. Asking questions such as, "Which piece do you like best?" "Which piece do you think is most significant?" "What is it about this piece that intrigues you?" "Can you add/take away/change a part of this to make it more direct/subtle/poetic/lively?" help students to delve deeper into their reactions to a piece. Such interaction supports students without taking away their ownership of the work.

Stage Five: Publishing the Scrapbook

At this point, students have reworked the materials they want included in their scrapbook. They are now ready to design their work, taking into consideration elements that will most complement the material, for example, placing a photographic essay on a black background, having their scrapbook professionally bound, or including illustrations that support the text. As well, they can prepare introductory and closing sections, for example, a table of contents, a foreword, and a conclusion.

Stage Six: Sharing with an Audience

There are several ways in which students can share their autobiographical scrapbooks. If there is a fairly even distribution among cultures explored in the scrapbooks, students can form a small group (an optimum number of members is five). Each group has one class period in which its members can share their work with the rest of the class. If there is an uneven distribution, each student can make a short presentation to the class. A third method involves students sharing their work as a member of a small group. In this instance, each group comprises members who have explored a different culture. In this way, all students are exposed to other cultures.

Exploring Culture Through Group Reading Experiences

The second activity builds on the research, writing, and presentation skills students developed when preparing their autobiographical scrapbooks. In this activity, they are asked to form groups to explore a culture other than their own.

The focus in this activity is placed on group reading experiences involving novels, short stories, poems, plays, and content selections. Through this reading, students are provided with a means of investigating the lives of their contemporaries from other cultures and other parts of the world. Discovering aspects of a culture — its customs, folklore, art, music, language, artifacts, and values — lead students to a deeper appreciation of the culture and its unique place in our world.

Given the scope of this project, groups often find that they can best convey the essence of a culture through the presentation of one or two aspects, for example, its literature or its traditions. This helps to define and shape the amount of information presented in the final product.

The success of this activity depends, in great measure, on the quantity and quality of support materials the students will employ. They need to understand the importance of this aspect of the activity, and that they will have to devote time and attention to library research. In addition to the materials noted above, you can also alert students to materials they would not normally use. One such example is that of picture books, which often deal with mature topics in a manner accessible to all students regardless of language ability. The wide array of choice within this genre makes a visit to the picture book section of your school and local library rewarding for all students.

Organizational Concerns

There are several ways in which students can organize themselves for this activity. They can form small groups (no more than five members) based on a culture or geographical region that they would like to explore. If a large number of students are interested in the same culture or region, they can form several groups. Group members then decide on how they will research materials related to their topic. When finished, they pool their materials and pass them around the group, with each student reading one or two pages of each selection. Students record their interest in the selections by assigning them a score from 1 (low) to 10 (high). When all students have finished reading the selections, they determine as a group the assignment of reading materials.

If students are undecided on a culture or region they wish to explore, provide them first with several titles that focus on regions around the world. In the same fashion, they read the first pages of the selections, ranking them on a score from 1 (low) to 10 (high). They can then conduct their own library research, bringing to the class selections that focus on several cultures or regions that interest them. Once they have rated these materials, students can share them with others who are also having difficulty deciding. When students have read pages from a range of selections, they can make their choice as to what they will explore based on the interest and appeal of the samples they read. Students form groups with others who are interested in exploring the same culture or region.

Assessment and Evaluation Criteria for Group Reading Experiences

As in the first activity, both the process and the product are valued. I have found that students' performance as a member of the group is best marked out of 20. This mark takes into account the extent and enthusiasm of each student's participation (process). The remaining 30 marks are reserved for the final group presentation (product). The presentation, like the process, should be marked holistically using criteria developed by both yourself and the students. The presentation mark can be based on a combination of your mark and that of peers, or based solely on peer evaluation marks. Sample criteria for presentations can include:

- clarity of presentation,
- extent of research,
- subject knowledge,
- participation of all members,
- creativity of presentation.

Opening the Reading Response Log

In this activity, students use their logs as a triple-entry notebook (first introduced on page 97). On the left-hand side of the page, students summarize what they have read by recording discoveries they have made, facts they have uncovered, and questions they have about the text. On the right-hand side of the page, they respond by generating questions, sketching scenes, relating how they feel about what they have learned, and making suggestions to themselves regarding further reading. They leave space in the margins where their group members can respond to the material in the log.

To begin work with the log, I usually read aloud some of the literature, and ask students to respond to what they have heard in their logs. Although it may not be necessary, you can use response starters such as, "What does this story remind you of?" "How do you feel about what happened in the story?" and "What do you notice about the customs and practices of the characters?" I have found that at this stage students are so comfortable with the process of reader response that the task can be left open-ended. When they are finished, students can participate in a group share where they discuss their thoughts and their log responses with others in their group before joining the rest of the class.

A Three-Stage Process of Exploration

As a large group, we discuss the schedule for this activity, dividing it into three stages:

Stage One: Reading
Stage Two: Researching
Stage Three: Presenting

We select dates that are agreeable to all of the groups, and sign up for presentation times. All groups, of course, are given the same amount of time for the three phases. Students record the schedule in their logs.

Stage One: Reading

The reading requirement is that each student is to read at least one text from the selected category. For some students, this will be more than enough while for others they will want to read several selections.

Students will need approximately five to seven classes in which to read their text. At the beginning of each class, students meet with group members in a literature circle where they share their responses and relate their reading. They discuss the schedule and check that all members are on track with their reading. Students should try to keep the literature circles to a maximum length of 10 minutes so that they have sufficient time for in-class reading.

When finished, students can meet in their literature circle to discuss and summarize their reading. The following prompts can help students generate discussion on the texts:

• How did reading this selection change your way of thinking?
• What did you learn?
• What do you still feel you have to learn?
• What is the one fact that you have learned from this selection that you would most like to share?

Through immersion in short stories, novels, poems, magazines, newspapers, essays, and journals, students experience a taste of the life of people in many cultures. Their logs will comprise their responses to the material they have read, as well as the responses of their group members. With each reading and response, students' definition of what constitutes a culture continues to be shaped.

I encourage groups to create a series of webs that detail elements of culture and the ways in which they have encountered these elements in their reading. Webs, written initially on chart paper, can be copied by each group member into his or her log. Common threads are discovered, ideas compared and contrasted. Just as the first activity increases students' sense of self and culture, this activity increases awareness of the fact that we live in a multicultural society where barriers between countries and continents are fast disappearing.

Stage Two: Researching

Together, students plan the resources they will use to investigate their culture or region, including books, videos, films, pictures, magazine articles, and artifacts. If students are not experienced in citing references, this is an ideal time to hold a mini-lesson on the topic. A class chart, on display throughout the research period, can serve as a reminder to students of the need to cite sources in their work.

In their groups, students divide the tasks and create a group schedule for completion of research. Students can record findings from the research in their logs, continuing the format of the triple-entry notebook as they examine news articles, read stories, essays, and letters, find pictures, and conduct interviews. By the end of the research period, their log begins to resemble an anthropologist's collection of thoughts. Students can use the log as a tool for thinking about the culture and as a source of data needed to assemble the learning for presentation.

Stage Three: Presenting

Drawing on their members' reading — literature and non-fiction selections — groups are now ready to work toward a multimedia presentation that will be shared with other groups in the class. Questions they can use to guide their presentations include:

- What have we discovered about this culture?
- What are the important cultural influences on the lives of teenagers in that culture?
- How do the contexts in which the people live define who they are?
- What are the common threads of the culture?

Again, the image is one of a collage or mosaic, echoing the nature of multiculturalism. In their groups, students work together to present a portrait of the culture they have investigated. Sources of information they can use include novels read by members of the group, newspaper and magazine articles, poems, and essays, and films and videos they have watched.

Students use mixed media to present their information. While they can select any number of ways to introduce and inform their peers about the culture they have studied, students should determine the optimum modes of presentation. The time frame allotted to the presentations will determine their character.

Some possibilities for presentation include:

- using video clips of daily life, traditions, celebrations and so on,
- displaying picture albums,
- role playing a celebration,

- telling a story,
- re-enacting a typical dinner conversation,
- preparing maps,
- drawing diagrams and pictures,
- displaying posters,
- displaying artifacts and explaining their significance,
- playing live or recorded music,
- reading poetry aloud,
- reading a letter aloud,
- displaying relevant newspaper and magazine articles,
- acting out or describing traditions,
- telling traditional stories.

Another approach may be to sponsor a multicultural festival. Students prepare a booth to house products that showcase their knowledge. To view the work of their classmates, students can sign up for a tour of the booths, or several small groups can band together to present their work simultaneously.

Concluding Remarks

We wrote this book to invite teachers to join readers and literature through active engagement with texts. We read student logs and heard the literary discussions. In the process, we increased our appreciation for the diversities that enrich our classes and worked to make our invitations into literature even more compelling. The longer we teach the more we learn that we cannot presume to know what individual readers will find significant, nor prejudge what previous knowledge and experience they will bring to a text. What we have presented provides each of us with the means to generate contexts that allow literature reading and response to develop and flourish — for a lifetime.

In case you're curious: at the end of the school year, Ed and his peers did indeed write the government exams. They had spent the year preparing — reading, writing, talking, and listening. They had been immersed in the reading and writing process, had talked through issues, and made meaning together. Were they prepared? Indeed. And, I might add, Ed got the highest mark in the school. I still smile when I think about it!

References

Atwell, N. 1987. *In the Middle: Reading and Learning with Adolescents*. Portsmouth, NH: Boynton Cook Publishers/ Heinemann.

Barnes, D. 1992. *From Communication to Curriculum*. Portsmouth, NH: Boynton Cook Publishers/Heinemann.

Barnes, D., & Todd, F. 1995. *Communication and Learning Revisited: Making Meaning Through Talk*. Portsmouth, NH: Boynton Cook Publishers/ Heinemann.

Berthoff, A. 1981. *The Making of Meaning: Metaphors, Models, and Maxims for Writing Teachers*. Portsmouth, NH: Boynton Cook Publishers/Heinemann.

Cazden, C. 1988. *Classroom Discourse: The Language of Teaching and Learning*. Portsmouth, NH: Boynton Cook Publishers.

Chambers, A. 1996. *Tell Me: Children, Reading and Talk — How Adults Help Children Talk Well About Books*. York, MA: Stenhouse Publishers/Markham, ON: Pembroke Publishers.

Cormier, R. 1991. *I Am the Cheese*. New York, NY: Dell Publishers.

Dias, P., & Hayhoe M. 1988. *Developing Response to Poetry*. Milton Keynes, UK: Open University Press.

Emig, J. 1983. *The Web of Meaning: Essays on Writing, Teaching, Learning, and Thinking*. Portsmouth, NH: Boynton Cook Publishers/Heinemann.

Fulwiler, T. (ed.) 1987. *The Journal Book*. Portsmouth, NH: Boynton Cook Publishers/Heinemann.

Garfield, L. 1967. *Smith*. London, UK: Constable Young Books Ltd.

Hughes, T. 1967. *Poetry in the Making: An Anthology*. London, UK: Faber & Faber.

Hunt, R. 1982. "Towards a Process-Intervention Model in Literature Teaching" in *College English, 44*, 345-357.

Jones, P. 1988. *Lipservice: The Story of Talk in Schools*. Milton Keynes, UK: Open University Press.

Langer, J., & Applebee, A. 1987. *How Writing Shapes Thinking: A Study of Teaching and Learning*. Urbana, IL: National Council of Teachers of English.

Lowry, L. 1993. *The Giver*. Boston, MA: Houghton Mifflin Co.

Moore, B., & Booth, D. 1988. *Poems Please! Sharing Poetry with Children*. Markham, ON: Pembroke Publishers.

Newkirk, T. 1989. *Writing and Thinking: Reclaiming the Essay*. Urbana, Il: National Council of Teachers of English.

Orwell, G. 1945. *Animal Farm*. Orlando, FL: Harcourt Brace & Co.

Parsons, L. 1994. *Expanding Response Journals*. Markham, ON: Pembroke Publishers/Portsmouth, NH: Heinemann.

Paton, A. 1940. *Cry, the Beloved Country*. New York, NY: Macmillan Publishers.

Pike G., & Selby D. 1988. *Global Teacher, Global Learner*. London, UK: Hodder and Stoughton.

Rief, L. 1992. *Seeking Diversity: Language Arts with Adolescents*. Portsmouth, NH: Heinemann.

Rosenblatt, L. 1938, 1983. *Literature as Exploration*. New York, NY: Modern Languages Association of America.

Staton, J., Shuy, R., Peyton, J., & Reed, L. (eds.). 1988. *Dialogue Journal Communication*. Norwood, NJ: Ablex Publishing Corp.

Tiedt, P.L., & Tiedt, I.M. 1990. *Multicultural Teaching* (3rd ed.). Boston, MA: Allyn & Bacon.

Watson, K. 1987. *English Teaching in Perspective*. Washington, DC: Taylor & Francis, Inc.

Wells, J., & Hart-Hewins, L. 1992. *Read It in the Classroom: Organizing an Interactive Language Arts Program*. Markham, ON: Pembroke Publishers/Portsmouth, NH: Heinemann.

Wyndham, J. 1993. *The Chrysalids*. New York, NY: Carroll & Graf.

Index